Are You a Regular Guy?

A Guide to Being a Man in the '90s

by

Lee Stratton

DORRANCE PUBLISHING CO., INC.
PITTSBURGH, PENNSYLVANIA 15222

ISBN # 0-8059-3300-X
Printed in the United States of America

First Printing

DEDICATION

This book is dedicated to my parents, Russell and Claire Stratton, who brought me up to be regular, and to my wife, Adele, who has allowed me to stay that way.

ACKNOWLEDGMENTS

A lot of people, some unwittingly, helped me with this book. My heartfelt appreciation to:

Lori Schwartz and Judy Grossman of Edelman Public Relations for their patience, guidance, and encouragement and especially for dealing with the fancy-pants attorneys and corporate bigwigs so that I wouldn't have to.

Paul Sklar, Aqua Velva brand manager, for his many suggestions.

John Friend, John Switzer, Bob Ruth, Dennis Feily, Bill Eichenberger, Joe Blundo, Mike the barber, Billy the bartender, and Joe the bus driver, who, either by suggestion or example, helped me define the regular guy.

I'd also like to thank the *Columbus Dispatch*. The idea for this book grew out of a column I wrote for the *Dispatch*. Several other ideas – how to improve baseball and college mascot match-ups – also appeared under my *Dispatch* by-line.

CONTENTS

Introduction: Are You a Regular Guy?

STAR
DINER

What Is a Regular Guy?

We are vindicated. No, more than that, we are victorious!

After enduring a decade of sneers from guys in BMW luxury sedans, suspenders and Gucci loafers, we find the shoe is on the other foot. Regular guys have become the men of the '90s.

Those men of the me-first, want-it-all generation are on the wane. After filling their closets with fine clothes, filling their garages with expensive cars and filling their stomachs with nouvelle cuisine, they found that they were unfulfilled. They found their expensive playthings didn't make them happy.

I could have told them that. I have been perfectly happy wearing suits that cost less than some guys pay for fountain pens.

I tried to give them clues that they were on the wrong track. For instance, one guy I know made a regular habit of checking the time on his new and expensive Rolex watch in my presence.

"What time does your new and expensive Rolex watch say?" I'd ask.

"Nine-fifteen," he'd reply.

"That's funny. That's the same time my old, cheap Timex has, too."

Timex is a regular guy watch just as Aqua Velva is a regular guy after shave. That's what regular guys wear, you know—after shave. They don't wear men's fragrances that sell themselves as "distinctively masculine" or "reflecting the essence, aura, and success of today's man." These fragrances also sell themselves for about $30 an ounce—the price of a decent set of socket wrenches.

Regular guys don't feel the need to smell successful or spirited. Regular guys are satisfied to not smell bad.

We would rather smell a freshly caught trout frying over a campfire, the newly spaded earth in a backyard garden, or the beer-and-smoke musk of a neighborhood bar.

Regular guys are neither trendy nor the Archie Bunkers of the world. The regular guy is your average, down-to-earth fellow. He enjoys helping out with Little League, Boy Scouts, and community projects. He's willing to help a neighbor move a refrigerator or a stranger start a stalled car.

The regular guy knows it's more important to spend time than money on his kids. He works hard and isn't afraid to get his hands dirty.

He hates to shop. But he likes to tinker around in one. The regular guy tends to be handy around the house.

He loves his family, his country and his sports. He knows a lot more about the Bulls and Bears of Chicago than the ones on Wall Street.

Being a regular guy isn't a matter of money. Sam Walton of Wal-Mart fame, one of the richest men in the world, doesn't give a hoot about appearances. He's regular. Donald Trump is not.

Regular guys like regular food – meatloaf, pizza, mashed potatoes and gravy, spaghetti and fried chicken. They see no sense in paying extra for extra-small portions, or for fish that hasn't been cooked.

The regular guy looks for the good in people instead of just looking for good-looking people.

He's a decent guy who appreciates having a decent job that pays a decent wage.

He doesn't want it all. It would be too much of a hassle to take care of. But, occasionally, he does want to get away from it all. Whatever he wants, he doesn't *have* to have it now. He's willing to work for it.

He's a back slapper, not a back-stabber. And, if you really need it, the regular guy will give you the shirt off his back. Just don't expect it to be Perry Ellis. He's most comfortable in jeans and sweatshirts.

The regular guy can be somewhat stubborn. He has his way of doing things. He doesn't like to change – even when he knows it's for the better.

Regular guys get their hair cut, not styled. Their dogs don't have styled hair either. A springer spaniel, retriever or mutt is a typical regular-guy dog. An Afghan hound is not.

Regular guys don't need a telephone-equipped, four-wheel-drive off-road vehicle just to cruise the freeways between exclusive neighborhoods and reserved parking spaces downtown. If a regular guy is driving a truck, chances are, he's on the way to a construction site or a hunting cabin in the woods.

And don't assume that all men in the woods are regular guys. Some fellows from the so-called men's movement of the '90s are out there beating drums, chanting, squatting in sweat lodges, and lamenting about how their fathers never taught them how to be men.

These guys aren't regular, they're confused.

That's why I've written this book. I want to help. For those who aren't sure whether they are regular, this handbook may help them decide. For those of you who know you aren't regular, but want to be, maybe it will help show you the way.

But be forewarned. It's easy *being* a regular guy. But it isn't easy *becoming* one. Most regular guys come by it naturally.

I know some guys aren't going to make it or even try. They'll continue tooling around in BMWs, talking on car phones, and trying to look more important and richer than everyone else.

I feel sorry for them. They are obviously suffering from irregularity.

Are You a Regular Guy?

Take this quiz to determine your standing in the regular guy world.

SECTION A
MULTIPLE CHOICE

1. The last tickets I bought were for
   a. a concert
   b. a cruise
   c. a ball game

2. The word "French" reminds me of
   a. French Riviera, French doors, and French horns
   b. French cuffs, French pastries, and French kisses
   c. French fries, French toast, and French bread pizza

3. To me, Kiwi is
   a. a bird I saw in New Zealand
   b. a delectable fruit served at business luncheons
   c. a good brand of shoe polish

4. In the trunk of my car is
   a. I'm not sure—ask my driver
   b. a set of golf clubs
   c. a set of tools

5. At noon, I
   a. do lunch
   b. drink lunch
   c. eat lunch

6. During the Gulf War, I
   a. worried about the price of oil
   b. worried about travel restrictions
   c. worried about our boys overseas

7. When I want to gamble, I
   a. fly to Vegas
   b. play the market
   c. chip in on a lottery ticket with the guys at work

8. When I hear the word "banana," I think
   a. banana daiquiri
   b. Banana Republic
   c. banana split

9. I think Ivan Boesky was
   a. smart for getting rich
   b. dumb for getting caught
   c. third baseman for the Dodgers

10. My bathroom scale
   a. tells me my weight in digital numbers
   b. tells me my weight in an electronic voice
   c. hasn't been out of the closet since Reagan became a Republican

11. A well-outfitted man has
   a. a pocket secretary
   b. a pocketbook
   c. a pocketknife

12. The song goes: "Mommas, don't let your babies grow up to be ____________"
    a. chubby
    b. Democrats
    c. cowboys

13. When I was a kid I collected
    a. precious stones
    b. protection from the smaller kids
    c. bottle caps, rocks, and baseball cards

14. When I show off my favorite baseball card, I say
    a. I paid $2,000 for this guy's card.
    b. I'll sell it in a couple of years and get twice that much.
    c. I was there the day he scored the run that won the pennant. It was a night game. Dad and I had seats right along the third base line. I can still remember the crack of the bat....

15. If asked to use the word "junk" in a sentence, I would say
    a. I'm completely divested of junk bonds.
    b. no junk food for me. I'm watching my cholesterol.
    c. I'm going to the junkyard to get a transmission for the Chevy.

16. When some guy drives by in a BMW, I think
    a. "upscale"
    b. "uptown"
    c. "up yours"

17. The word "power" makes me think of
    a. power lunch
    b. power politics
    c. power tools

18. Last night I told my son
    a. don't mix your Bugle Boy and Calvin Klein clothes in the same drawer.
    b. not now. I've got these reports to read.
    c. go out ten yards, cut left, and I'll hit you with a pass.

19. Last night I told my daughter
    a. O.K. If you have to have a diamond tennis bracelet like Bitsy's, we'll get one tomorrow.
    b. I've hired a string quartet for your birthday party.
    c. go out ten yards, cut left, and I'll hit you with a pass.

20. Last night, I told my wife
    a. if you'll pick up my shirts at the cleaners on your way to work, I'll stop by the Gourmet Shoppe on my way home and pick up dinner so you will have time to take Suzie to her ballet class on your way to the league meeting. I'll drop Justin off at his soccer match on my way to my tennis date with Skip. The kids will have to find rides home with friends so you and I can meet my new client at the club for a couple of drinkypoos.
    b. I'm calling from the car. The incompetent jerk at the Gourmet Shoppe put the wrong kind of pâté in the order. It's going to throw our whole agenda off tonight.
    c. great meatloaf, honey. Now I'm gonna watch the game on TV.

21. Last night my wife told me
    a. I just have to have more closet space.
    b. not now. I've got these reports to read.
    c. wake up and go on up to bed. The game ended a half-hour ago.

SECTION B
TRUE OR FALSE

__ 1. The Mudville nine are still in prison.

__ 2. My off-the-road vehicle has never been off the road.

__ 3. Jumper cables are a kind of exercise equipment.

__ 4. A socket wrench is a sports injury.

__ 5. My hardware won't work without software.

__ 6. All my clothes have the labels on the inside.

__ 7. Except for when I was in the military, I've always worn my hair this way.

__ 8. Every time I come home my kids ask, "What did you bring me?"

__ 9. The last time I got firewood, it was wrapped in plastic.

__10. They're called hip boots because the trendy people wear them.

SECTION C
WHAT IF

1. If I were a tree
   a. I'd be mahogany
   b. I'd be a weeping willow
   c. they'd call me "stumpy"

2. If I were a bed
   a. I'd be a water bed
   b. I'd be a flower bed
   c. I'd be a flatbed

3. If I were a ball
    a. I'd be a charity ball
    b. I'd be a tennis ball
    c. I'd be a bowling ball

4. If I were a book
    a. I'd be a bankbook
    b. I'd be a cookbook
    c. I'd be a comic book

SECTION D
WORD ASSOCIATION

1. "Broker" reminds me of
    a. stockbroker
    b. real estate broker
    c. my financial condition, compared to yesterday

2. "Pool" reminds me of
   a. swimming pool
   b. secretarial pool
   c. football pool

3. Complete the word: "Astro_____"
   a. naut
   b. nomical
   c. Turf

4. I am most likely to be seen in
   a. a yacht club
   b. a night club
   c. the Elks Club

5. I am most likely to be in
   a. a hot tub with my date
   b. Hot Springs with my parents
   c. hot water with my wife

HOW TO SCORE

SECTION A

Give yourself 2 points for each time you answered c. Deduct 2 for each time you answered b. Deduct 5 for each time you answered a.

Note: Answer c on question 9 is regular, but incorrect. Ivan Boesky didn't play baseball. You're probably thinking of Shawn Boskie, who pitched for the Chicago Cubs. Give yourself 10 bonus points if you knew his 1990 ERA was 3.69.

SECTION B

Give yourself 2 points for each time you answered false on questions 1-5. On question 1, give yourself 5 bonus points if you said that Casey should have bunted when he was at bat.

Give yourself 2 points for true answers on 6 and 7 and for false answers on questions 8-10.

Also on question 10, give yourself 5 bonus points if you thought, "I ought to be wearing hip boots now—this guy's spreading it deep."

SECTION C

Follow the same scoring as in Section A.

SECTION D

Same as Sections A and C.

Total up your points.

OTHER BONUS AND PENALTY POINTS

Add 10 points if you took this test with a pencil.

Add another 5 points if you unconsciously moistened the pencil point on your tongue as you worked.

Deduct 20 points if you used a fountain pen—50 points if it's gold.

Deduct 100 points if you told your administrative assistant to take the test for you. Deduct another 50 if he passed it on to the student intern.

THE RESULTS

115 points—In this case, a perfect score means you're NOT regular. You're lying. Nobody's perfect. But you apparently want people to think you are. Regular guys aren't afraid to admit to a few mistakes.

80 points or more—Get yourself a beer and go back to watching the game. You've got nothing to worry about. But you already knew that because regular guys don't worry about some silly test in a book.

50-79 points—Go watch the rest of the game, then continue reading. You've got regular tendencies but you've got a lot to learn. There's still hope for you.

-400-+49 points—Close the book. Go on a cruise. You're in for a long decade.

Sports

"I just wanna catch the score, hon."

Sports Watch

A regular guy loves to talk about his favorite team when it's winning almost as much as he loves to complain when it isn't. That's why there are still regular guys living in Cleveland.

Regular guys are the happiest sitting in a stadium where they watch a game, drink beer and yell.

They are almost as happy sitting in front of the TV at home where they watch a game, drink beer and yell. In fact, some regular guys prefer watching games at home because:

- You can't take your dog to the stadium.
- You can't sit in a stadium in just your underwear.
- Other regular guys won't know if you doze off during the third quarter.
- You don't have to wait in line at the rest room.
- You don't have to wait in line to get a beer.

Even at home, regular guys take their sports seriously. That's why most of them have TV sets in the basement. "Hank," the regular guy's wife says, "I don't care if it was third and two or how big of a jackass you think Sam Wyche is, I'm not going to have you frightening the children like that. Now get down off that table, pick up the magazines you threw, and go watch the game in the basement."

Just because a sporting event is on television doesn't mean it's regular. You can nail a regular guy to a chair in front of a TV, but he'll still refuse to watch gymnastics or figure skating. A regular guy will occasionally watch a non-regular sport, such as bicycle racing, but only if he thinks the American team has a good chance of beating the Russians or French.

Regular Sports

One measure of the regularness of a sport is the amount of protective equipment the players need. Helmets, face masks, pads and protective cups are all good clues that this is a regular sport. Here is a guide to what's regular and not regular in sports:

Football—Very regular. Lots of hitting and grunting on the field and yelling and jumping in the stands. Fans can yell at the players during each play, at the coach after each play, and at the referees the rest of the time. Requires massive amounts of protective equipment and a strong work ethic. A player will play with broken bones and torn muscles. That's regular.

Hockey—Even more regular. Much like football, but the players wear blades on their feet and carry sticks. About the only time the game action stops is for a fight. Plus there's always that element of danger from being hit by a puck, a drunken fan, or even one of the players who didn't like what you yelled.

Baseball—Regular with yuppie leanings. It still offers plenty of opportunity to watch games, drink beer, eat hot dogs and yell at the umpires. But unlike football, too many baseball players get paid outrageous salaries and whine about sore fingers. Regular guys don't understand that. A pair of seats cost more than a pair of shoes and can be so far away from the playing field that they have different zip codes. One other thing. Some stadiums have become so trendy they've started serving sushi. People who eat sushi at a baseball game are not regular. They're not even to be trusted.

Auto Racing—Regular. Particularly stock cars and dragsters. The drivers wear asbestos suits. Regular guys have had love affairs with cars since their teens. You can yell at a drag race all you want. You can even yell insults at the guy standing next to you. It doesn't matter. Nobody can hear a damn thing.

Golf—Not regular. Too prissy. Players pay someone to carry their equipment. They also wear plaid pants, pink shirts and shoes with tassels. They play all day without getting their clothes dirty. You can't yell at a golfer even though he is swinging at a ball that is sitting perfectly still. Baseball players hit balls traveling more than 90 miles an hour while thousands of fans roar.

Tennis—Not regular. Much like golf. Any sport that restricts the fans to polite applause after a great shot is not regular.

Soccer—Not regular. It doesn't make sense. Lots of running and kicking but very little scoring. Regular guys will watch it only when their own kids are playing. Then they still don't understand it.

Basketball—Regular. Fast. Exciting. Slam-dunk. Michael Jordan. Enough said.

Boxing—Very regular. There's nothing more manly than two guys, toe-to-toe, slugging it out, even though most regular guys think a lot of it is fixed by the mob. Plus you can argue forever about whether a recent boxer like Ali could have beaten Louis or Marciano.

Softball—Regular. Close enough to baseball to be respectable with enough differences to be playable. Even an older regular guy can hit a ball lobbed underhand. Lots of hitting, running, and yelling during the game. Lots of beer drinking afterwards.

Bowling—Totally regular. Lots of noise and a real sense of power when those pins go flying. Plus, you get to drink beer *during* the game.

Volleyball—Semi-regular. It's okay if it's played at a picnic or as a get-up game. But beach volleyball is definitely not regular, especially in the Midwest where they truck in the sand.

Touch Football—Touch football is for regular guys even though the Kennedys play it. It's also one of the few times regular guys touch each other.

"I think I finally got the hang of this game."

If We Could Play Hardball With the Owners

Every few years regular guys are put through the ordeal of baseball contract negotiations.

Baseball players and their agents threaten to strike if they don't get what they want—namely, more money. Baseball owners and their lawyers threaten a lockout if they don't get what they want—namely, more money.

But it's the fans who are left out in the cold during the process. And when it's all over, the regular guy is the one who usually ends up having to sacrifice something—namely, more money. Ticket and concession prices keep going up.

If the fans could hire an agent for the next baseball contract negotiations, here are some things regular guys would ask for:

- Alcohol-free zones in every stadium for kinder, gentler fans
- Free-alcohol zones for the rest of us
- Hot dogs that don't cost like they are pedigreed
- Wave insurance to cover the cost of spilled beer and popcorn
- A pay-for-performance clause—ticket prices should go down with the team's performance
- A free-agent rule for fans—once a team falls below .500, a fan could declare himself a free agent and trade in the remainder of his season tickets for those of a better team
- Ballparks with natural grass
- More day games so kids could cut school like the good old days
- An extra stretch in the fourth inning
- Better score cards
- Better scores
- Giant video screens that show *Field of Dreams* when the game gets dull
- A ban on players who become involved in drugs, paternity suits, and underwear ads
- A three year limit on a manager's permission to say, "This is a rebuilding year"

Things to Take to the Game	Things to Leave at Home
1. Thermos bottle	1. bottles of mineral water
2. binoculars (the ones you use for duck hunting will do)	2. pom poms (regular guys just shake their fists)
3. miniature radio with earplug to hear other scores	3. hand-held TV (they are too small to be of any value)
4. sweatshirt, jacket, or waterproof coat with a hood	4. sport coat and tie
5. warm, waterproof boots (the ones you use for duck hunting will do)	5. Gucci shoes
6. hat (either stocking or a gimme) in your team's colors	6. umbrella (it blocks the view and drips on the guy in front of you)
7. tickets	7. cellular phone
8. the family, a buddy, or a date	8. anyone who's wearing a sport coat, tie, or Gucci shoes
9. cash for hot dogs and parking	9. credit cards (the hot dog and beer vendors don't accept them)
10. sandwiches for tailgate party before the game	10. Lunch from the caterer with china and cloth napkins

Bears, Buckeyes, and Banana Slugs

Although regular guys are ardent baseball fans, they're just plum crazy over football. They love every part of it, from the crunch of helmets, pads, and bones on the field to the dancing cheerleaders, the crazy names, and the costumes that have evolved over the years. Which brings up the question, where did they get those names, anyway?

People in Columbus, Ohio, get a little touchy when you refer to the Ohio State University Buckeyes as a "bunch of nuts." But that's what a lot of folks, especially University of Michigan fans, think Buckeyes are.

Of course most teams have regular mascot names such as Bulldogs, Tigers, Lions, Eagles, or even the Fighting Kangaroos. They sound tough and aggressive, which is what a sports team wants to be.

Ohio State isn't the only school with a not-so-regular nickname. There are the New York University Violets, the Whittier College Poets, and the Nazareth College Moles. And don't forget the Banana Slugs of the University of California at Santa Cruz. What could be lower, more repulsive, and less threatening than a yellow slug? What coach wants a sluggish offense?

This is one example why California isn't a real regular place.

Regular guys take their college team mascots seriously. They display them on hats, sweatshirts, sweaters, and windshield decals. During the games they bark like bulldogs, roar like tigers, and yell things like, "Hook 'em horns," and "Roll Tide," "Go Blue," and, oh yes, "Go Bucks."

You can tell if the school is regular if the fans are bare chested (in 20° weather), painted from head to toe, waving swords in the air and yelling things like "Kill 'em! Make the quarterback eat that damn ball!"

The school is not regular if they are waving white hankies in the air and yelling, "Repel them, repel them. Make them relinquish the ball."

There could be some interesting match-ups if football bowl games or basketball tournament bids were based on team nicknames. Here are some examples:

The Chivalry Bowl

Knights vs. Dragons

(Queens College & Tiffin U.)

The Ford Classic

Thunderbirds vs. Mustangs

(Southern Utah State & Southern Methodist U.)

THE JUSTICE BOWL

Judges vs. Vandals

(Brandeis U. & U. of Idaho)

The Harvest Bowl

Cornhuskers vs. Haymakers

(Nebraska & Phillips U.)

THE SHAFT BOWL

Orediggers vs. Claimjumpers

(Montana Tech & Columbia College)

The Big Tree Classic

Foresters vs. Lumberjacks

(Huntington College & Humboldt State U.)

The Mud-Ugly Invitational

Horned Frogs vs. Gila Monsters

(Texas Christian & Eastern Arizona College)

The Big Blow

Hurricanes vs. Cyclones

(U. of Miami & Iowa State)

The Great Write-Off

Penmen vs. Poets

(New Hampshire College & Whittier College)

Communication

Regular Guy Talk

Regular guys talk regular. We don't have meaningful dialogues. We say what we mean. We don't use any of those highfalutin words used by a lot of professors, bureaucrats, and fancy-pants executives.

We don't "expedite the process." We "cut through the bull."

Regular guys start a lot of conversations with a favorite word—"Howbout"—as in "Howbout those Vikings" or "Howbout them Cards."

Regular guys talk about a wide range of topics—high school sports, college sports, professional sports, indoor sports, and outdoor sports.

One other thing. You can call a regular guy by his first name or just his last name. You can call him "pal," or "old buddy," or "my friend."

But he doesn't like to be called "dude." He doesn't like to be called by computers. And he doesn't like to be called late for lunch.

Speak Up

Regular guys don't beat around the bush. They don't dress up their language any more than they dress up themselves. Regular guys say:

- "job" not "career"
- "sewer maintenance workers" not "effluence enhancement engineers"
- "die" not "pass on"
- "garbage men" not "sanitation engineers"
- "janitors" not "maintenance engineers"
- "hospitals" not "trauma centers"
- "bartender" not "mixologist"
- "trucks" not "over-the-road transporters"
- "get off a plane" not "deplane"
- "plumber" not "aquatic systems service technician"
- "undertakers" not "eternal life planning consultants"
- "a chewing out" not "a work performance motivational consultation"

You can't fool a regular guy by talking about revenue enhancements. He knows a tax hike when he sees one.

Straight From the Horse's Mouth

Regular guys season their speech with terms from sports, work, and the great outdoors:

- Someone who is wrong is "way off base."
- Taking on a challenge is "tackling a problem."
- Someone knowledgeable of the situation "knows the score."
- If you are in trouble, "your goose is cooked."
- If it's time to make a decision you've got to "fish or cut bait."
- Regular guys tell impatient people to "hold your horses." Of course, if there's a good reason to hurry, well then, "that's a horse of a different color."
- Someone who is angry is "madder than a wet hen."
- And a regular guy who sits down to a breakfast of bacon, eggs, home fries, and biscuits is in "hog heaven."
- Some people are "about as useless as tits on a boar hog." Others are "horned-toad ugly" or "dumber than a mud fence."
- Guys who work hard all day are "dog tired" or "tuckered out."

Regular guys get a lot of work out of the word "dead."

- Someone with good aim has a "dead eye."
- Someone who doesn't work is a "deadbeat."
- If he drinks too much, he is "dead drunk."
- If you are out to get him, he's a "dead duck."
- Guesswork is "dead reckoning."
- The regular guy who is opposed to something is "dead set against it."

*"You mean we were interfacing...
I thought we were just flappin' our jaws"*

Words Regular Guys Don't Use

1. *Mode* – "I'm in a relaxation mode right now."
2. *Spiffy* – "Those are real spiffy vice grips you have there, Frank."
3. *Downscale* – "I'm going to downscale the height of this hedge."
4. *Utilize* – "I'm going to utilize my pocketknife to downscale my fingernails."
5. *Facilitate* – "That linebacker should facilitate the quarterback's inability to run the ball."
6. *Upscale* – "I see you bought the upscale model of the toilet plunger."
7. *Input* – "Hey ump! Why don't you get some input from a seeing eye dog?"
8. *Outplacement* – "The university's board of trustees ought to offer the coach some outplacement opportunities."
9. *Demographics* – "Whooee! Look at the size of that defensive line. The demographics are all wrong for a quarterback keeper."
10. *Fuchsia* – "Now I want your honest opinion. Do these fuchsia gloves clash with my camouflage pants?"
11. *Interface* – "Put your butt down here on the bar stool, Duke. I want to interface with you about the Bears."
12. *Implement* – "I've implemented a new policy. I'm not going to drink anymore. I'm not going to drink any less, either."

Ten Things You'll Never Hear a Regular Guy Say

1. Oh, well. It's only a game.
2. I can't go fishing with you tomorrow, Bill. I have an appointment at the tanning salon.
3. Hey, I've got an idea. Let's go to the mall.
4. You've really got to give credit to those guys in Washington.
5. Let's see. For lunch I'll just have a frozen yogurt and some carrot sticks.
6. I'm really counting on your support to help me be appointed chairman of the social committee.
7. Honey, are you driving the Beamer or the Mercedes convertible to work?
8. Great news, honey. I just called the ticket broker. I was able to get tickets for the opera tonight.
9. Hey, did somebody take the lifestyle section of the paper this morning? I can't find it anywhere.
10. It's almost the end of the second quarter. What say we leave early and pop over to the club?

Regular Guy Jokes

Just about any guy can tell a joke. But a regular guy can take a joke, too. That's one of the reasons he's fun to be around. We don't take ourselves too seriously. That's why you'll find us joking *about* the psychiatrist's couch instead of *using* it.

Regular guys joke about women, sports, hunting and fishing, sex, and anything that isn't regular. Mostly we tell our jokes to other regular guys who won't be offended.

A regular guy doesn't share his jokes with his wife very often because she is likely to snort and say something like, "That's gross. When are you guys ever going to grow up?" Another reason is that he usually has forgotten them by the time he gets home.

A typical regular guy joke goes:

My wife said if I go fishing one more time, she's going to leave me. Gawd, I'm gonna miss that woman.

A regular guy might tell his buddies:

A feminist was on the Donahue Show this morning complaining that men do all their thinking below the belt. My wife liked that. She said that must be why I'm so short-sighted and narrow minded.

Things He Will Joke About

- ✓ Himself
- ✓ His wife
- ✓ His in-laws
- ✓ The government
- ✓ Non-regular guys
- ✓ Politicians
- ✓ Rival sports teams
- ✓ Hairdressers
- ✓ College professors
- ✓ Golfers

Things He Won't Joke About

- ✗ His friend's dog
- ✗ His wife when she's present
- ✗ His mother, present or not
- ✗ His friend's daughter
- ✗ POWs and MIAs
- ✗ The flag
- ✗ His favorite teams
- ✗ Cancer
- ✗ The real big guy at the bar
- ✗ His first car

More regular guy jokes:

A regular guy was sitting in a bar when a gorgeous young woman sidled up to him. She was wearing a very tight, low-cut, extremely short dress which revealed her abundant charms.

"Hello there, handsome," she said. "Would you like to buy me a drink?"

"Sure," he gulped. He drank in her lusciousness as she drank down the gin.

Finally she put her hand on his leg and said, "Let's not beat around the bush. I'm good, but I'm expensive. For $50, I'm yours for half an hour. For $200, I'm yours for the night."

"What would you do for $500?" he asked.

"Anything you want," she cooed.

"Anything?" he asked.

"Yes. Anything," she breathed.

"O.K., here's $500. I want you to paint my house."

* * * * *

Then there was the guy who went to his doctor and complained of feeling depressed, sluggish, and just not interested in doing much of anything.

After giving him a complete physical, the doctor said, "Well, nothing shows up on the tests. But I think I know what's wrong. You realize you're getting older, and it's bothering you.

"I went through the same thing a while back. But I found a great way of getting over it. I had sex with my wife every day for a month. You ought to try it."

Some time later the guy was back in the doctor's office.

"Did you do what I recommended?" the doctor asked.

"Yeah. It was great. And by the way, I like your house, too."

* * * * *

One evening a guy and his secretary have to work late at the office. When they finish, they go out for some drinks together. One thing leads to another and they end up at her condo where they make mad, passionate love and fall asleep. At about 3 A.M., he wakes up, throws on his clothes in a panic and races across town. A few blocks from his house, he stops in front of Clancy's, an all-night pool hall. He runs inside, rubs chalk dust on his suit and then drives home.

His wife launches into a tirade the moment he walks through the door. "Wait," he says. "Let me explain what happened. I took my secretary out for drinks after work. We drank too much, went back to her condo and ended up making love. I fell asleep, woke up at 3 A.M., and came right home. And that's the truth."

"Yeah, right," she says sarcastically. "Look at the front of your suit! You've been down at Clancy's playing pool all night."

Regular guys love to tell sports jokes—especially when they can get in a couple of digs at rival fans.

For instance: A Yankees fan might tell a Cleveland Indians fan this story:

Pete Rose was seen at an Indians game. "What are you doing here?" a fan asked.

"Just what the commissioner ordered. He told me to get as far away from professional baseball as I could."

Jokes about college football arch rivals are always rampant in the fall. For instance, an Oklahoma fan might ask:

"What did God say when he created Arkansas students?"

"Act dumb until I get back to you."

If a Regular Guy Had Written It...

- A bird in the hand means you're a good shot.
- Laugh and the world laughs with you. Cry, and you belong on the "Donahue" show.
- Go ahead. Make my meat loaf.
- Play it again, Sam, and you'll see he caught that ball out of bounds.
- A penny saved isn't near enough.
- April showers bring muddy boots.
- The best things in life are not on TV.
- An apple a day tastes better if it's in a pie.
- Half a loaf is better than no rest at all.
- What this country needs is a good, 5-cent nickel.
- Hell hath no fury like Bobby Knight losing.
- All work and no play means you've got my job.
- The early bird gets shot first.
- Early to bed and early to rise and your girl goes out with the other guys.

- If I had a hammer, I'd fix that downspout.
- Give me Liberty or give me Orange. Any bowl game will do.
- You scratch my back, and I'm in deep trouble with my wife.
- There's no fool like an old Senator.
- You can't have your cake and your figure, too.
- He who lives by the sword will be no match for a 12-gauge.
- Hello, young lovers. You're under arrest.
- Go West, young man. Just stop before you get to San Francisco.

Appearance

LOU'S
HI-FI
AQUA-VELVA

Rise And Shine

Regular guys don't take bubble baths. We don't use bath oils or a 7-step hair-care system. Regular guys think that "mousse" is French for a large, antlered animal found in the North woods.

We don't primp or pamper or dally in front of the bathroom mirror. A little deodorant and some after shave are about the only luxuries we allow ourselves.

When we get up in the morning, getting ready to go out isn't any more complicated than getting ready to stay in.

A shower, once-over with the razor, and a splash of Aqua Velva after shave about does it.

We don't use any designer fragrances—wasting that much money early in the morning would put us in a bad mood for the rest of the day.

Most regular guys take showers instead of baths. If God had meant for regular guys to take baths, he wouldn't have put showers in all the locker rooms and army barracks. Showers are quick and efficient. You don't waste water and you don't waste time waiting for the tub to fill.

We're not fussy about the stuff we wash with either. We use whatever soap and shampoo our wives buy. Single regular guys use whichever ones their mothers always bought.

Some regular guys shower before they shave so the water softens their beards. Others shower after they shave so the water washes the blood away.

After a shower, we dry our hair with a towel and comb it. The only split ends we worry about are the ones on the football team.

We don't change our looks with the trends and times. We get our hair cut at a barber shop, not styled at a salon. And we get it cut the same way we've always worn it since high school, except for the time we were in basic training in the military. Nobody, not even a regular guy, wears his hair that short by choice.

Regular Guys Don't Dress by Design

It's not difficult to pick the regular guy out of the crowd. He's the one who isn't in a hurry. Everything about him is relaxed, even his clothes.

He's not the one trying to impress everybody with a $500 suit. He dresses to suit himself. Usually, that means a flannel shirt or t-shirt, jeans, and tennis shoes. And he doesn't put on airs—Nike shoes or otherwise.

He's the one with starch in his character, not in his shirt.

He doesn't have moussed hair or pierced ears. He goes to a saloon, not a salon. He doesn't have a diamond tie pin, earring, or pinky ring, gold cuff links, gold chains, or jangly bracelet. His only jewelry may be a plain wedding band and perhaps a service club lapel pin. He wears the wedding ring only because it makes his wife happy.

He doesn't carry a purse or wear any kind of scarf. To him "Gucci" is something you say to a baby, not something you wear. His clothes don't have polo ponies, crocodiles, boars, swans, or tigers on them—but they are made in America.

Let's get down to basics. A regular guy likes his clothes to be functional, not fancy. He wants something that is going to last.

Regular guys don't buy underwear that comes on hangers—it comes three to a package and gets bleached, not dry cleaned.

We wear the same outfits almost everywhere—to games, restaurants, scout meetings, and parties. If we have to change clothes, we don't want to go.

At night we take off our clothes and sleep in our underwear. Regular guys have one pair of pajamas and a flannel robe for overnight stays at the in-laws'. We have a pair of slippers that the kids gave us for Father's Day a number of years ago.

The regular guy has one or two suits to wear to church, weddings, and funerals. He has them cleaned once a year.

He doesn't own a tuxedo. He rents one probably no more than two or three times in his life—for his senior class prom, for his wedding if he didn't elope, and for the weddings of any of his daughters who don't heed his advice to elope.

The regular guy hates to shop for clothes.

He makes this pilgrimage only when his wife insists because the cloth is completely worn away on his shirt collars, cuffs, elbows, and tails. The buttons have been replaced two or three times and the zipper on his pants is missing several teeth. The last time coins fell down through his pants leg, he patched the pocket with duct tape. By the time he's done with his old duds, even the Salvation Army doesn't want them. That's how bad he hates to shop.

When he finally gives in and goes shopping, he does it this way: He goes to one store, finds one shirt and one pair of pants—both wash-'n'-wear—that fit his body and his wallet. Then he asks the clerk to get him two more of the exact same thing, only in different colors.

"Now honey, you promised you'd look for some new underwear."

Some regular guys are required to wear shirts and ties to work. If so they usually work with their collar open, the tie loosened, and their shirt sleeves rolled up two or three turns. It's as relaxed and comfortable as they can get under the circumstances. This is a regular guy look.

Back in the '70s, politicians caught on to this and adopted the look so that they would appear regular, too. They appeared in TV commercials with open collar, loosened tie, and rolled-up sleeves, walking through a farmer's field while looking up at the sky and talking about keeping America clean, green, and great.

They didn't fool *real* regular guys. Regular guys know that you don't look up at the sky when you walk through a cow pasture.

Keeping a Cool Head

If the regular guy has a trademark, it's his hat.

Regular guys wear those baseball-style caps with the cloth front, mesh back, and adjustable size. They are about as practical as a guy could want, plus you can get them free as promotional items.

In a lot of areas, they're called "gimmes," because when a regular guy sees one he likes, he says, "Gimme one of those."

When he gets one, he adjusts the size and bends the sides of the bill down a little bit. That gives the hat real regular character.

The more regular the hat's logo, the more likely he is to want it. John Deere, International Harvester, Smith & Wesson, Pabst Blue Ribbon, and Aqua Velva are coveted gimmes. Louis Vuitton leather sun visors are not.

Regular guys don't wear hats that have to be blocked. Blocked hats are for blockheads.

A Tip of the Hat to the Regular Guy

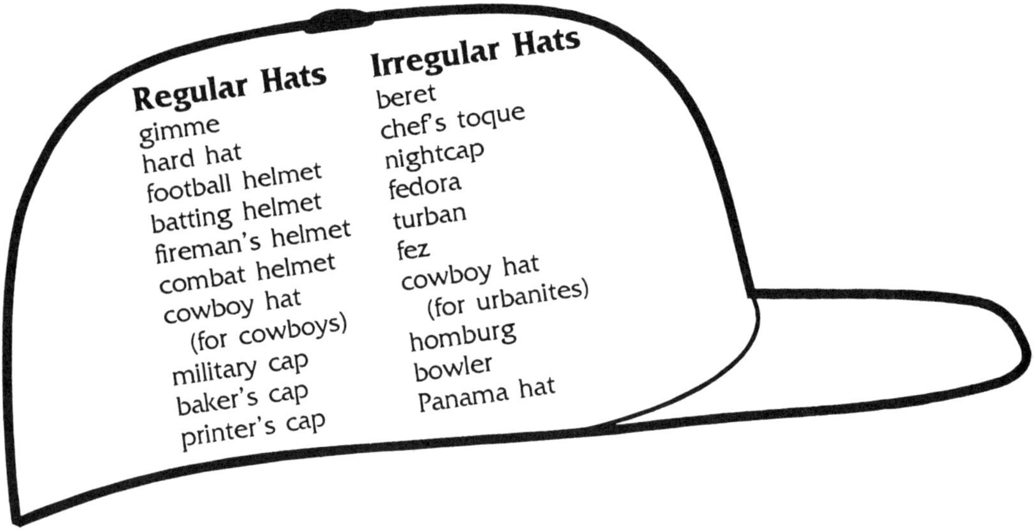

School

WASHINGTON ELEMENTARY SCHOOL

3rd Grade Midterm Report

STUDENT: Robert Simpson **DATE:** March 20

SUBJECT	GRADE
Reading	C
Math	B
Spelling	C
Science	C
English	C
Physical Education	A
History	B
Music	C-
Art	D+

Comments:

Robert is a pleasant child to work with and I enjoy having him in my class. He does well in reading as long as the stories are about baseball or animals. He particularly enjoyed "Sounder". However, he showed little interest in completing the assigned book report on "Toby's Adventure at the Mall."

Most of us enjoyed Robert's history report on the life of Daniel Boone. However, a little more guidance from home would help avoid another unfortunate incident such as his graphic directions on how to skin and cook a rabbit. Some of the other children were quite traumatized.

Robert's spelling is improving. But he still insists on spelling "socks" as "sox". He says that's the way they spell it in Chicago and Boston. Please help me straighten him out on this.

Mrs. Quidmore, the art teacher, would like for Robert to expand his use of colors from just the basic brown, black and green. Everything he draws looks like it came straight out of a G.I. Joe comic book.

– Mrs. James

Parent's Signature ____________________

The A-B-Cs of Being Regular

From elementary school through college, the regular guy shows a lot of regular traits. He's interested in learning practical information, not something that sounds impressive at a cocktail party.

He doesn't take acting classes in high school or college. He already knows how to act. He just acts natural.

He teaches his family, just as he was taught, that a good education is one of the most important things a guy can have.

He may not have been the star student in the classroom, but he has learned a lot of things at the hands of the best teacher of all – experience. He knows it's just as important to know how to read the opposing offense or a pressure gauge as it is to know how to read a stock table.

Washington High

GOOSE,
YOU ALWAYS GAVE IT YOUR BEST AND WAS A GOOD TEAM PLAYER. KEEP MAKEING ME PROWD!
—COACH JOHNSON

Robert,
I know you are the one who started calling the Glee Club the Tee-Hee club. But I'll remember you because you intervened when the jocks wanted to de-pants me in the gym.
Best wishes for the future - Melvin

ROB MY MAN,
WHAT CAN I SAY? AFTER I GET MY MBA, I'LL LOOK YOU UP. I'LL NEED SOMEONE TO TUNE UP MY CAR (PORSCHE OF COURSE!!!) HA!! - Biff

Goose,
I'll never forget the awesome excuses you forged on the 1st day of hunting season. Good Luck in Boot Camp.
Your Good Buddy "Tombstone"

SANDRA "Sandy" SIMMONS
College Preparatory Course
Debating Club,10,11,12; Glee Club ,9, 10,11,12; Science Club,11, 12; French Club,10,11,12; Players Club, 9,10,11,12; Class Secretary 9, 10; School Adm. Asst.11,12; Young Republicans 11,12; president 12; Voted Senior Class "Most Political" and "Nicest Hair"

Hey buddy!
Hang in there.
Moose

BOBBY!!!
I'M GLAD WE GOT TO KNOW EACH OTHER!
CHEERS FOR WASH HIGH!!!
REMEMBER ME ALWAYS!
:-)
BUFFY

School Yearbook

Sweetheart—
I think I'll cry forever.
How can these days be
over? I'll wear your
class ring all thru nursing
school & always cherish our
song & the times we drove
to "The Point" + let the air
out of the tires on Biff's
convertible! Thanks for the
grad gift - a dozen
hankies will really
come in handy!
Love forever
Cindy
XOXOXO

ROBERT "Goose" SIMPSON
General Studies Course,
Football 9,10,11,12; co-captain, 12; Track,10,11,12; Varsity Club, 10,11,12; Kingpin Auto Club, 11,12; president,12; Bowling Club, 10,11,12; Voted senior class "Most Friendly Guy" and "Most Likely to Still Be Eating Pizza When He's 80".

GOOSE!
NEVER SELL
THE "ROAD
BEAST!" WHAT
A CAR! DON'T
FORGET THE
GANG -
RED DOG #27

Bob,
Best gun rack in all my
shop classes! Keep up the
good WORK!
Mr. Jenkins
(PS PLEASE RETURN THE 35 PLUGS YOU REMOVED FROM
the Power
tool cards!)

Basic Training

Regular guys really aren't impressed with scholars and academicians whose lives are all a matter of degrees. Someone may boast of having a B.S., M.S., and a Ph.D. The regular guy thinks, "Well, we all know what B.S. stands for. M.S. is just "more of the same," and Ph.D. stands for "piled higher and deeper."

A lot of regular guys go to college. But we don't make a career out of it.

We're most likely to go to agriculture schools, technical colleges, or state universities. We shy away from liberal arts colleges and the Ivy League. We're more apt to major in geology than psychology; forestry than botany; animal science than political science.

We are unlikely to study art, global economics, home economics, sociology, human ecology, or philosophy. And regular guys definitely don't major in theater. That program is like granola – nothing but fruits, nuts, and flakes.

We may major in education – the physical variety.

Outside class regular guys are more likely to join ROTC than social fraternities because they haven't had the prerequisite course, "Snobbery 101." They don't see any good in it and they don't understand it. A regular guy just says, "It's all Greek to me."

Regular guys usually live together in dorms or apartments. They play college or intramural sports. They take dates to the football and basketball games. On spring break they usually go home, not to Jamaica.

Some regular guys never finish college. They go to work to earn tuition money and find out they learn more useful stuff on the job where the teachers are regular guys, too.

Jobs

BUS
STOP

Working Men

Work isn't a four-letter word to a regular guy, regardless of how it's spelled.

He's a good man for the job, as long as the work is regular and steady. He considers it a good job, even if the work is hard and dirty. He's more apt to carry a lunch box than a briefcase.

He may complain about his job. But he hates to miss a day of work, even when he's sick. Being under the weather is no excuse not to be out in it.

When he's on the job, he knows what he's doing and takes pride in doing it.

Good work is his trademark. It's the regular thing to do.

What We Do

The first thing a guy wants to know about a new acquaintance is, "Who do you root for?" The second thing is, "What do you do?"

After his family, work is life itself to the regular guy. It's not only what he does, it's what he is. He may beef about the difficulty of the work, the ineptness of the bosses, and laziness of his peers. But he gets the work done. He would be lost without it.

Regular guys don't flit from one job to the next. When we find a decent one, we hold on to it and beef and bitch and work—everyday. We don't call in sick because of the sniffles, a headache, a backache, or a stomachache. We don't just put in our time. We put in a good effort.

Regular guys tend to work for companies with no more than two names. A regular guy's employer is more likely to be Peterson and Sons than Frederick, Farley, Folsen, and Farquire.

Regular guys work in a lot of places, from coal mines underground to the tops of utility poles or skyscrapers.

You'll find regular guys down on the farm, up on the housetop, out on the range, or in on the assembly line.

We're a lot more likely to deal with livestock than blue-chip stock, backhoes than back taxes, hardware than software. If we work with students, it's probably in high school, not college.

Regular guys frequently carry a lunch bucket instead of a briefcase. Regular lunches are two sandwiches instead of two martinis.

If we work in an office, we are more likely to have a work station, not a credenza. Our desktops are littered with work, not electronic gizmos and executive toys. We keep things in piles instead of files. Our paper clips are silver, not lavender, chartreuse, or umber.

Our few distractions include office jokes and football pools.

Take a look at the guy next to you. If he's a regular guy, you'll see that he's been working hard instead of hardly working.

As a newspaper reporter, I've heard a lot of regular guys tell some pretty funny stories about their jobs.

For instance, there was the locksmith who was called in the middle of the night by a restaurant manager.

"We've lost the keys, and the locks need to be changed right away," the manager said. The locksmith did the work and was paid in cash on the spot. The next morning, the owner of the same restaurant called the same locksmith and asked him to come and install new locks. "My manager got into a snit and quit last night. The S.O.B. changed the locks, and I'm locked out of my own restaurant."

One of my own favorites involves my first newspaper job in a small town in southern Ohio. I found out that the county sheriff had just purchased a bunch of shotguns with a federal grant that was supposed to be used for non-lethal weapons, such as tear gas and rubber bullets to be used in civil disturbances.

The sheriff justified bending the rules by saying, "My deputies have wanted new shotguns for a long time. We don't need non-lethal weapons."

The morning after my story ran in the paper, the telephone on my desk rang.

"You Stratton?" the man on the other end of the line asked.

"Yes, that's me."

"You're new down here, ain't ya?"

"Yes I am. Why?"

"Well, there's something you need to understand. A shotgun in the hands of a Ross County deputy *is* a non-lethal weapon."

Jobs No Regular Guy Would Take

1. hair stylist
2. manicurist
3. insurance salesman
4. stock broker
5. tax auditor
6. concert flutist
7. TV news anchor
8. gourmet chef
9. obstetrician
10. male stripper
11. flower arranger
12. decorator

Jobs They Would Take Instead

1. tree trimmer
2. dock hand
3. fireman
4. bronco buster
5. taxidermist
6. Dixieland tuba player
7. TV cameraman
8. donut baker
9. delivery man
10. mail carrier
11. farmer
12. deck hand

In Sickness...

Regular guys don't call in sick, even when we are. We leave standing orders with the family to not call the doctor unless we've been unconscious for more than two days, are unable to crawl half the distance to the bathroom, or are so delirious with fever that we answer the phone and say yes to a free Arthur Murray dance lesson.

When regular guys get sick, we try to "tough it out." We keep ourselves going with aspirin, antacid, or any over-the-counter remedy that promises to dry you up at either end.

When we're too sick to get out of bed, we don't whine and complain. We just want to be left alone.

No regular guy likes spending the day at home without getting anything done around the house. And it doesn't make us feel any better when we turn on the TV and find that instead of a ball game, "Donahue" is on with cross-dressing clergymen who want to marry recovering chocoholics and adopt striking Greyhound bus drivers as their children.

Stuff like that is enough to make you *really* sick.

"A free Lambada lesson? Sure, why not."

Common Regular Guy Maladies

1. sore back from lifting the Rototiller into the truck
2. fish hook in the back of the neck
3. chapped hands from washing off grease with gasoline
4. spark burns from the cutting torch
5. mashed thumb from hammering
6. splinters from football bleachers
7. bruised shin from splitting firewood
8. sore knees from weeding
9. tongue burn from five-alarm chili
10. beer farts

Uncommon Maladies

1. carpal tunnel syndrome from keyboard use
2. champagne cork in the eye
3. paper cuts
4. burn from the tanning booth
5. sprained toe from kicking the golf cart
6. tennis elbow
7. creative burnout
8. writer's block
9. cramped fingers from signing American Express charge slips
10. flattened ears from constant car phone use

Relationships

Regular Romance

A regular guy isn't exactly the type to sweep a woman off her feet with romance. He's more likely to give her a broom for her birthday.

Being gooshy, mooshy, and sensitive isn't his style.

If he remembers, he'll give his girlfriend flowers or candy on her birthday, or both after being told he forgot. The flowers are usually carnations from the supermarket. The candy comes from there, too.

On Valentine's Day he gives her a card, but nothing frilly, lacy or intimate to go with it. He would rather eat nails and be dragged naked through the middle of town at high noon than be caught in a Victoria's Secret store.

He never recites poetry to his love, much less writes poetry, unless he forgets to buy a card. Then he'll fold a piece of typing paper in half and write something like:

Violets are blue,
Roses are red,
Since they're $50 a dozen,
I made you this card instead.

Or to his wife:

It's Valentine's Day
I married a winner!
Here's your card,
What's for dinner?

Hint to all you regular guys: You'll be really lucky to get away with this once. If you do, don't try it again.

A regular guy shows his true love by sharing the things he loves with his woman. Things like football and hockey tickets. If he thinks the world of her, he'll include her in the activities he shares with his friends. Things like pizza and beer on Friday nights or their touch football game on Sunday afternoons.

If he's really hooked, he'll wrestle with her on the living room floor during a break in the action on TV. This is not an attempt at forced sex. It is just his way of showing he cares. If he lets her win, once in a while, it's his way of showing he *really* cares.

If he's head-over-heels, slam-the-barn-door-Katie in love with a woman, he'll reveal the depth of his innermost feelings by saying something like, "You're something else, ya know that?"

Then, and only then, will he offer to share one of his most cherished, and most private treasures. He'll let her come along to his favorite fishing hole.

"True love"

Where He Takes a Date	Where He Doesn't
neighborhood bar	the opera
a hockey game	the symphony
on a picnic with friends	the ballet
his softball game	a foreign film
her softball game	any place that requires a coat and tie
his place for a game on TV	a cocktail party
her place if she has ESPN	an art gallery
tractor pulls at the fair	a Beaux-arts ball
the drag races	any event that serves drinks in glasses with stems
out for pizza	a poetry reading
a bowling banquet	any event where there's an ice sculpture

There She Is, Mrs. Regular

The regular guy isn't looking for a homecoming queen or Miss America. He's looking for "a good woman" to share his life.

She doesn't have to enjoy hunting or fishing or camping or sports as long as she doesn't try to keep *him* from enjoying them. She only has to be tolerant in that respect.

He doesn't care if she watches "Oprah" on TV just as long as she doesn't go on the show and talk about him.

The regular guy hopes his intended will agree to elope. He doesn't want a fancy affair. But if she insists on a wedding, he expects her to accept his friends with open arms, even if they do show up without ties. And she must accept that there will be beer alongside the champagne at the reception.

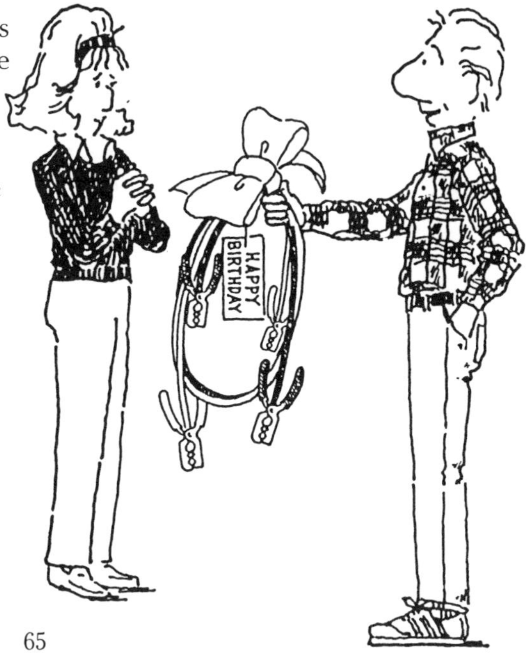

Qualities a Regular Guy Appreciates in a Woman

The ability to make meat loaf
The willingness to cook fish

A sense of humor
The sense to be quiet when a game is in overtime

A respect for work and money
A respect for the simple things in life—especially him

The ability to keep him going when he's down
The ability to keep him down when he's going too far

The maturity to jealously guard their relationship
The maturity to not be jealous of his relationship with his dog

The strength to wrestle with problems often
The desire to wrestle with him occasionally

Heartbreak Hotel

It's hard to believe that a man whose attributes include loyalty, reliability, and fidelity could end up divorced. But it happens. And he's usually the one who's the most surprised when it does. The regular guy is totally bewildered over why it happens. "I thought we were perfectly happy," he tells his pal over a beer at Ralph's Bar.

He was. She wasn't.

Her complaints aren't ones of him gallivanting around the country having his picture taken with starlets, models, or bimbos.

No. She complains that he's home *every* night—night after night. He's not verbally abusive, but "he just sits there for hours without saying anything." She says the only time he talks about his feelings is when he says, "I feel hungry," or "I feel like watching the Eagles instead of the Bears."

The main reason a regular guy ends up divorced is that he marries a non-regular woman who expects something more than a faithful companion. She wants her man to have more pizzazz, drive, and flamboyance.

This raises the question of why she married the regular guy in the first place. He didn't deceive her by suddenly changing from a fast track joy boy into an ordinary Joe after saying, "I guess I do." With a regular guy, what you see is what you get. She saw and she got.

The problem is that she secretly planned to change him after they married. She was going to make him sensitive, ambitious, even dapper.

That was her *big* mistake. You can't change a regular guy. He's set in his ways. Like concrete. With a regular guy, you not only get what you see, you're stuck with it, too.

To avoid this problem, there are some tip-offs a regular guy should look for in the women he dates. They are dead giveaways that she's a princess in disguise:

1. At a ball game, she does her nails instead of watching.
2. She doesn't like your friends.
3. You don't like hers.

4. She orders white wine instead of beer at a Pizza Hut restaurant.
5. She misses your home run in the softball game because she's talking on her cellular phone.
6. She wants to take you shopping for clothes.
7. She wants to make appointments for you with her hairdresser.
8. You can't identify any of the food she packs on a picnic.
9. Her bowling shirt has a designer label.
10. She gives you a briefcase, a $30 bottle of cologne, or red bikini underwear.

Houses

U.S. MAIL
The FENTONS

A Man's Home is His Castle

When a regular guy says, "A man's home is his castle," he's speaking figuratively. Regular guys don't live in castles or manor homes. Our homes are ranch houses, duplexes, or cape cods.

Read on to learn more about where the regular guy lives – his house, his town. Learn a little about the joys of do-it-yourself home repair, and consider the solutions to an alarming problem. Top that off with a quick look at some of the fun things he does around the house and you should end up with a good idea of whether you could feel right at home as a regular guy.

This Old House

If your house is a very, very, very fine house with two cats in the yard, it's probably not regular. This handy checklist will help you determine if your house is too fine to be regular:

- A lived-in living room is regular. A great room is not.
- A front door is regular. An entry system leading into a great hall is not.
- A first floor, second floor and basement are regular. A main level, loft and balcony are not.
- A bathroom with a shower-tub combination is regular. A whirlpool tub on a raised platform is not. (Regular guys don't like to bathe on stage.)
- Parents' bedroom is regular. A master suite is not.
- A doorbell-triggered security camera is not regular. Chimes that play the Notre Dame fight song are.
- A utility room is regular. An electronic control center for the "smart wiring" is not. (A regular guy doesn't want wiring that's smarter than he is.)
- A three-car garage, hot tub, an electric gate across the driveway, an in-ground sprinkling system, and an olympic-size heated swimming pool aren't regular.
- A den is regular. A media room with a hidden, wall-size TV screen connected to three VCRs and movie theater sound system is not.
- A rusty set of barbells under the workbench is regular. A basement gym with enough chrome to make Ray Charles blink isn't.

Our Town

You just know that some towns and cities are more regular than others. Boise has got to be more regular than Palm Beach or Palm Springs.

Some towns just *sound* more regular than others. For instance, Pea Ridge has a lot more regular name than Society Hill.

In general, small towns are more regular than big cities. But big cities have the big sports teams.

Here are some things that make a town or city regular:

- smokestacks
- professional sports teams within driving distance
- summer softball leagues
- a decent bowling alley
- a decent steak house
- a decent junkyard
- a reputation as a decent place to raise a family
- municipal parks
- mobile home parks

Among big American cities, there are some that could be considered regular. Here's why:

- ***Pittsburgh*** – The "Iron City" with a regular-guy work ethic. It also has the Penguins, the Pirates, and the Steelers.
- ***Chicago*** – The city with broad shoulders, lots of beef, deep-dish pizza, and the Bears, the Bulls, The Blackhawks, and two baseball teams, if you count the Cubs.
- ***Boston*** – A city of baked beans, Irish pubs, the Bruins, Red Sox, and the Celtics, and home of *Cheers*.
- ***St. Louis*** – Home of Anheuser-Busch, the maker of regular beer; the Arch, and the St. Louis Blues. It used to be home to two teams called the Cardinals; now they're down to one.
- ***Detroit*** – The place where regular cars and Motown music got their start. Also the home of the Lions, the Tigers, the Pistons and the Red Wings.
- ***Cincinnati*** – Famous for its chili, riverboats, coal barges, the Bengals and the Reds. Home of the first professional baseball game.
- ***Cleveland*** – Otherwise known for Lake Erie perch, ethnic neighborhood festivals, the Browns, the Indians, and the Cavaliers.
- ***Philadelphia*** – Home of the Liberty Bell, the 76ers, the Eagles, the Phillies, the Flyers, and Philly cheesesteaks and any other food covered with Cheez Whiz spread.

A Regular Guy's Perspective

Mr. Fix-It

Regular guys don't hire someone else to repair, remodel, rewire, maintain or install. We patch our own roofs, clean our own gutters, seal our own driveways, paint or wallpaper our own walls.

But we don't jump into these projects without forethought. Usually we think about a project for a year or two, or until our wives threaten to call "a professional" to get the job done. And once we get started, we often have second thoughts that drag out the project a considerable time longer.

"There, that oughta' do it!"

That's why in a lot of regular guy's houses, you're likely to see the same piece of woodwork is missing from the wall from one year to the next. Last year he stripped it. This year he'll stain and varnish it. Next year he'll decide it wasn't worth it and paint it to match the rest of the woodwork.

He generally does a pretty good job. Not as good as a pro, but pretty good. He shrugs off any imperfections by saying, "Well, that's close enough for government work," or "Hey, from downtown, who can tell the difference?"

A regular guy's neighborhood is like a biosphere for chores. What one regular guy can't do, another can. One is good with electrical things; he knows how to work an ohm meter and what to do with the red wire when the new ceiling fan directions just say "connect black to black and white to white." He helps his neighbor who returns the favor by loaning Rototiller equipment, a wheelbarrow, or posthole digger. They both help the guy down the street who has a chain saw and a long extension ladder.

Occasionally there's a job none of them can handle. At that point, one of them says, "I know a guy." The guy usually works for a company that specializes in the work you need done. He moonlights and charges about half of what his boss does – about what the job is worth.

If you want to be a regular guy, you're going to have to know a little bit about the tools and supplies needed for home repairs. Otherwise you could end up like the newlyweds who got their window caulk and K-Y jelly mixed up. You can imagine what happened to them. That's right! Their windows kept falling out.

The
I-Sent Away-for-the-Time/Life-Books Quiz
(A test of home repair knowledge)

1. Duct tape is good for
   a. sealing furnace pipe joints
   b. repairing the hem in your pant leg
   c. making swords and armor for the school play
   d. wrapping Christmas packages
   e. all of the above

2. A stud sensor
   a. is what my wife used to find me
   b. is not necessary if you have good knuckles and ears
   c. would have kept me from drilling 12 holes to hang that picture in the living room

3. I use a miter box to
   a. store leftover miters
   b. prop up the short leg of the workbench I made
   c. cut angles—but the woodwork in the corners still doesn't fit

4. Pipe dope is
   a. loose marijuana
   b. what my wife calls me when I try to repair the plumbing
   c. the stuff that gets smeared all over your pipe threads, shirt, pants and forehead

5. I need another extension
   a. telephone
   b. cord
   c. ladder
   d. to file my income taxes

6. Before using a keyhole saw, you should
   a. take the key out of the door
   b. take a week or two to think it over
   c. take the board over to your neighbor's house and ask him to cut it

7. Before wallpapering, you should
   a. send the kids away for their own safety
   b. make one last attempt to convince the wife that fresh paint would be just as attractive
   c. buy a couple of cases of beer and invite your buddies over for a wallpapering party
   d. all of the above

8. Finishing nails
   a. is a top priority in my personal grooming routine
   b. are the last two nails you use
   c. don't have heads and bend easily

True or False

__ 9. Furring strips are used to trim coats, hats, and rear-view mirrors.

__ 10. A caulking gun is accurate within 30 yards.

__ 11. A nail punch is what Ali used to knock out Liston.

__ 12. Black & Decker is an investment firm.

__ 13. Torpedo heaters are only authorized for Navy use.

__ 14. Glazing compound is used to frost daiquiri glasses.

__ 15. You can believe directions that say "can be installed in an afternoon."

__ 16. You can't cut corners with a circular saw.

Regular Guy Answers

1. E– Duct tape is the regular guy's all-purpose repair kit.

2. A– Regular guys think that's funny. Non-regular guys who can't find a stud at home, will just call up and order one from a catalogue.

3. C– But they're close enough for government work.

4. B&C– Regular guys aren't into drugs. A regular guy dropped some acid once. It ruined his shoes.

5. B&C– If you get a longer ladder, you'll need a longer cord, too.

6. B&C– Just make sure the neighbor has a 3/4-inch drill bit, too.

7. D– The paper party is a great idea. Guaranteed, you'll never be asked to paper again.

8. C– That's why regular guys buy them by the pound instead of in those little pre-packaged plastic containers.

9-16– If you answered true to any of these questions, you aren't regular and shouldn't try to do your own repairs. Hire someone or ask a regular guy for help.

Safe at Home

Regular guys aren't alarmists.

We don't have those high tech alarm systems in our homes that call the police, fire department or the Orkin exterminator every time somebody steps through the front door. We feel no need for a monthly check by a personal domain-protection technician.

Regular guys get by with a couple of well-placed smoke detectors and a window sticker that says, "This home protected by Smith & Wesson." We operate on the theory that "anyone found prowling around my property at night will be found there the next morning."

Regular guys also don't have alarms on our cars or trucks. We are annoyed with people who do. We are tired of hearing Beamers and Mercedes and other overpriced cars sitting on the street for hours with a siren whooping or the horn blowing and lights flashing. We are particularly disgruntled with people who put these alarms on four-wheel-drive trucks and jeeps. Any man who owns a truck ought to be man enough to protect it himself.

Any guy who leaves an alarm sounding for more than two minutes should be strung up by his Rolex watch. (Or locked in the car for 24 hours with a Barry Manilow tape playing.)

Home Life

Making a House a Home

All the things a regular guy does *to* his house aren't nearly as important as the things he does *at* his house—things like raising kids, raising vegetables and raising a little hell once in a while.

Spending time teaching and playing with his kids, entertaining friends with a cookout, tending to a garden—those are the things he puts his heart into. And when he has family and fun at home, it's easy to see that the old saying—"Home is where the heart is"—was written for the regular guy.

Kidding Around

The regular guy's philosophy about raising kids is the same as his philosophy about everything else – straightforward and simple:

Something like, "Raising kids is a two step process. You spend two years teaching them to walk and talk and the next 16 telling them to sit down and shut up."

Regular guys don't raise kids by the book. We raise them by the heart, by common sense and by example. We want our kids to grow up with character, not to be characters. We want them to accept responsibilities, care about others, and value work and achievement.

We want our children to be happy.

But most of all, what regular guys really want is for our children to grow up regular.

That's why you will see a lot of regular guys coaching ball teams, leading scout troops, and spending a lot of time with the family. That's also why they are more interested in getting their kids into 4-H clubs than into country clubs.

We'll work alongside our sons and daughters in community projects and take the time to teach them the things we know. Useful things like how to use tools, hit a ball, change a tire, solve a math problem, identify poison ivy, tell the difference between blue jays and bluebirds, or why it's important to pass on first down once in a while.

When there's a school project to be done, regular guys provide dowel rods, clay, and construction paper, not a computer program that does the project by itself.

Regular guys know that raising kids is the most important thing a dad can do. They also know that despite their best efforts, some kids are going to take off in the wrong direction. There might come that day when a teenager announces, "I want to go to Princeton, get an MBA, and land a high-paying job on Wall Street."

Experienced regular dads don't react with shock or a tirade at the rebellious teen. No. They'll look seriously at the kid and say, "Well, son, I'd like for you to go to Princeton. But I don't think the old station wagon can go that far."

Gender Benders

Regular guys give credit to the women's movement for one thing: girls are now allowed to sweat, thanks to their newly ordained involvement in organized sports.

The regular dad doesn't want his daughter playing varsity football or wrestling on the high school teams with boys. But a dad with all girls is no longer left on the sidelines while mom takes them to dance lessons, cheerleading, or Brownies. Now he can root for his daughter in softball, Little League, basketball, volleyball, track, and a host of other activities. Most anything the boys are doing, the girls are doing, too.

Unfortunately for dads with sons, the same is true in reverse. A lot of things the girls are doing, the boys are doing, too.

Nowadays dads find themselves saying, "No 7-year-old child of mine is going to have pierced ears! I don't care what the other boys are doing."

Things Regular Kids Won't Have

1. a big allowance for doing nothing
2. pierced ears in preschool
3. an imported convertible
4. a credit card
5. sleep-over dates
6. birthday parties that rival Ringling Brothers Circus
7. designer everything
8. enough electronic toys to cause a blackout
9. carpal tunnel syndrome from playing too many video games
10. a backyard gym set designed by Frank Lloyd Wright

Home on the Range

A regular guy is at home on the range a lot more than with the microwave.

He generally knows how to cook two or three things and he makes a big deal out of preparing them on certain occasions. For instance, it might be a once-a-year thing such as chili on Labor Day or ribs the day before the Super Bowl game. Or it could be a weekly thing—breakfast every Sunday.

Whatever it is, he's bound and determined to do it. He calls it a tradition. His wife calls it a nuisance.

Regular Guy Specialties

1. Steaks on the grill
2. Barbecued ribs on the grill with his own sauce
3. Barbecued chicken wings on the grill with his own sauce
4. Hamburgers, cheeseburgers, and hot dogs on the grill because the kids refuse to eat his own sauce
5. Chili
6. Venison stew
7. Pan-fried trout
8. Bacon, eggs, and home-fried potatoes
9. Fried bologna sandwiches
10. Fried green tomatoes

Things a Regular Guy Won't Cook

1. *Anything that requires a recipe*
2. *Anything that doesn't require chili powder, hot peppers, onions, or garlic*
3. *Anything that requires cookware other than a pot, kettle or skillet*
4. *Anything to be served on a bed of lettuce*
5. *Anything requiring the use of a whisk, a food processor, or toothpicks*
6. *Anything with yogurt or tofu*
7. *Anything involving bean sprouts*
8. *Anything that requires separating eggs*
9. *Anything that isn't likely to set off the smoke alarm*
10. *Anything that requires more than one serving to make you feel stuffed*

Good Guys are Seedy Characters

When regular guys want to get back to their roots, they dig up the ground.

Gardening is the way regular guys keep in touch with the rural, agricultural heritage of this great land of ours. There's something about digging in the earth, planting seeds, pulling weeds and watching the shoots turn into bean plants, and blossoms into pods, that makes a guy feel like he's accomplished something.

It's also good training for the kids. There's nothing like spending a hot, dirty day of pulling weeds, picking beans, and shelling peas to make them appreciate the advantages of a college education.

The regular guy grows regular things in his garden. You will find corn, beans, tomatoes, cucumbers, carrots, hot peppers, and onions, just to name a few.

He doesn't waste time or space on some exotic vegetable that no one has every heard of, let alone tasted. If he has to send away for the seeds, he isn't going to mess with it. He also won't plant things he doesn't like to eat. That's why there's no endive, eggplant, watercress, parsley, brussels sprouts, Chinese pea pods, or cilantro in his garden plot.

It doesn't take much to have a backyard garden. A lot of regular guys get by with a shovel, hoe, rake, some seeds, fertilizer, and water. The gardener is really well-equipped if he has a neighbor with a tiller.

If You Need These Things for a Garden, You're Not Regular

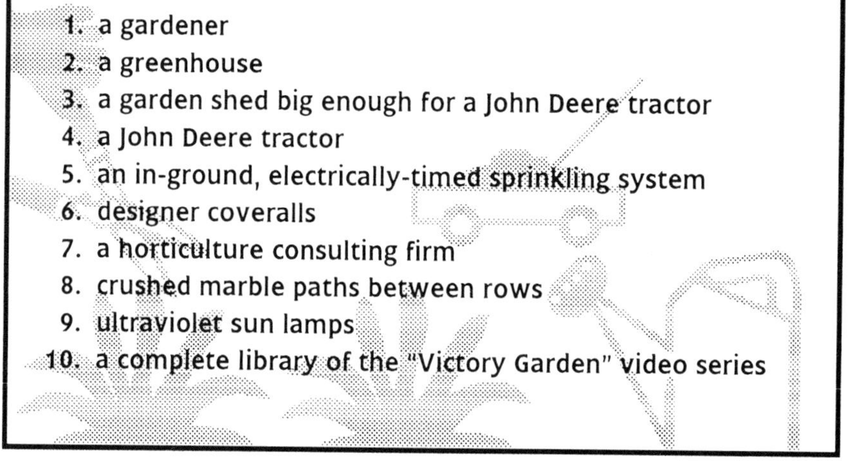

1. a gardener
2. a greenhouse
3. a garden shed big enough for a John Deere tractor
4. a John Deere tractor
5. an in-ground, electrically-timed sprinkling system
6. designer coveralls
7. a horticulture consulting firm
8. crushed marble paths between rows
9. ultraviolet sun lamps
10. a complete library of the "Victory Garden" video series

The Regular Guy World

Mr. Manners

The regular guy believes in old-fashioned courtesy.

The regular guy is the fellow who holds the door for women, older people or anybody with their arms full. He calls older women "Ma'am" and younger women "Miss."

He's not the guy who sends pedestrians scrambling out of the way as he sails through intersections while talking on his car phone and taking notes. No, the regular guy goes out of his way to give a local kid, a friend or a neighbor a lift home.

If someone wants to pull out of a parking lot into traffic, he'll leave a space. But if he's in stalled freeway traffic, he won't leave room for the guy in the BMW who drove along the berm to pass everyone else.

He's not the driver who turns red, uses blue language, and lays on the horn the split-second the light turns green.

If he doesn't have a disability, the regular guy doesn't take parking spaces marked for the handicapped, and he's never the guy who left the Fleetwood luxury sedan parked diagonally across two spaces in the parking lot.

If he sees someone has left their lights on while parked on the street or in the grocery store parking lot, he tries to turn them off.

He'll also lend a hand without being asked. If he sees a neighbor getting ready to climb a tall ladder, he'll go over and steady it. If he sees someone trying to move something heavy, he'll risk his back right along with them.

If he's the first guy out on the morning after a snow, he'll shovel the sidewalk in front of his house and those on either side of him. If older people or a single woman are neighbors, he'll do their sidewalks and driveways, too.

He's not the one who calls the police when pine cones fall into his yard from a neighbor's tree.

The regular guy is aware and considerate of his neighbor's goings-on. For instance, if a neighbor is having a family gathering and cookout, the regular guy will offer to lend a picnic table, grill, or folding chairs. He also will make sure his own grass is cut before the guests arrive and that there isn't any underwear hanging out on the line.

Please Don't Complicate Things

When the good Lord made regular guys he gave them an extra gene. The genetic code it carries is simple—K-I-S-S. It doesn't make them more amorous, but it patterns their approach to every aspect of their lives. Genetic scientists have isolated that gene and now know that the code it carries stands for "Keep It Simple, Stupid."

Tabasco sauce, not variety, is the spice of the regular guy's life. Simplicity is his guiding light.

He eats the same thing for breakfast every day, keeps the same schedule, lives the same routine, day-in, day-out. He keeps few clothes so he doesn't have to make a big choice of what to wear in the morning. He would like to live life with just one of everything. And everything would be a very few things.

This ordered approach to life is why little things such as, "Sorry, dear, we're out of oatmeal," really upset him. It's not that he likes the taste of oatmeal (a real simple food) that well. He just can't cope with the thought of changing to something else, even for one morning. It just ain't natural.

It's also why he hates TV specials. If "Hollywood's Glamour Boys Salute Themselves" is on instead of "Coach," it upsets the whole balance of his nature.

Simplicity, also, is why he sends his wife to the store for things he wants. It's not that he's lazy. It's just that stores aren't simple. The aisles and aisles of items are too overwhelming. They threaten to short-circuit the KISS code and blow his mind.

He is comfortable with his simple life, particularly when he's sitting in his own chair in front of the television. It's the same chair he sits in at the same time every night. Other people are allowed to use it when he's not there. But they generally don't because that's where the dog sleeps when he's gone.

He drinks out of his own coffee cup. Other people are not allowed to use it. It is oversized and has something like "World's Greatest Dad" written on it or a picture of a duck with the words, "Without my coffee, I'll quack up in the morning." He'll grumble for a year if a visiting relative happens to grab his cup off the shelf one morning before he can get to it.

Change – Who Me?

There isn't much a regular guy would change about his life. He has few regrets about the past. He's pretty happy with the way things are now. Besides, he doesn't cope with change very well.

He wouldn't trade his military experience for anything, even if he didn't particularly enjoy it at the time. It was the right thing to do. He wouldn't trade the lean years with his wife. Those were the good times. And he wouldn't trade the time with his kids for all the tea in China.

He would like to be able to go back and change a couple of things in high school – perhaps the block he missed in the fourth quarter of the league championship football game, or the cutting remarks he made about the class nerd.

He probably would like to change a couple of votes he cast for guys who seemed almost regular at the time, but ended up being real jerks.

Regular guys could always use a little more money because it would make things a little easier. But they don't believe a lot more money is necessary to be content.

But what if he won the lottery? He could live with it. Anybody can change some things about themselves. Even us regular guys.

If I Were a Rich Man (What He Would Do with Lottery Money)

1. pay off the house
2. paint the house
3. pay off the car
4. fix up the car
5. pay off college loans
6. donate just enough money to the college to qualify for good football seats
7. buy himself a bass boat
8. buy his wife a new mixer
9. buy a round of drinks for the guys
10. put the rest in the bank

That's Not Where My Money Goes (Things He Wouldn't Do If He Won the Lottery)

1. quit his job
2. allow the kids to quit theirs
3. buy a house in Palm Springs
4. buy a Lamborghini sports coupe with two phones
5. buy his kid's way into a prestigious school
6. buy a 60-foot cabin cruiser
7. buy his wife a mink coat
8. buy a round-the-world cruise
9. order one of everything in the Neiman Marcus catalogue
10. invest in the stock market

Rules to Live By

1. Play by the rules.
2. Keep your shoulder to the wheel.
3. You attract more bees with honey than vinegar.
4. Be satisfied with a good job, good family and good health.
5. Make all you can.
6. Save all you can.
7. Give all you can.
8. Moderation in everything.
9. Pull your share of the load.
10. When in doubt, punt.

Club Rules

Regular guys don't belong to a country club. We also don't belong to those stodgy, uptown clubs where men sit around and cut deals instead of cards.

However regular guys see nothing wrong with having clubs for men only. Women can have their own clubs or can have an auxiliary to the men's group. But let's face it, regular guys would be really embarrassed if a woman knew the silly things we do.

A lot of regular guys don't belong to well-known groups. But they'll form a club with fishing or hunting buddies. They give them fancy names like the "Trickling Springs Trout and Literary Society." They think it's funny.

Several times a year they head off to the woods together where they drink, fish or hunt, make wisecracks about each other, smoke cigars, play poker, and drink some more.

The only literature they read is the hunting and fishing reports posted at the live bait and ammo store, and maybe a couple of *Playboy* magazines that have been laying around the cabin for the past six years.

That's the whole club, except for the several other times a year when the guys get together in one of their basements to plan the next trip. During these planning sessions they drink, talk about fishing or hunting, make fun of each other, smoke cigars, and drink some more.

Groups like the Trickling Springs Bass and Literary Society have only a few rules:

- No women.
- No dues.
- No rules.

Regular Guy Groups and Organizations

- ▲ sportsman's clubs
- ▲ lodges with animal names like Moose or Elks
- ▲ American Kennel Club
- ▲ high school sports boosters clubs
- ▲ veterans organizations
- ▲ college sports boosters clubs
- ▲ local service clubs

Groups They Don't Belong to

- ▼ men's support groups
- ▼ bar associations
- ▼ animal rights groups
- ▼ Cat Fanciers of America
- ▼ Book of the Month Club
- ▼ symphony societies
- ▼ yacht clubs

Health Wise

Regular guys subscribe to the Ed McMahon school of thought on exercise.

On occasion Johnny Carson will ask, "Ed, do you jog?"

"No," Ed replies, "I have a man who does that for me."

Up-scale guys do it differently. First they pay out a lot of money to join a fancy club where they plan to exercise. But soon they find the membership is going unused. They might even join another club, closer to work or closer to home. But the only health benefit they derive is from carrying the weight of an extra membership card in their wallet.

Next, they spend a big chunk of change for a fancy piece of exercise equipment to use at home. Usually it's a rowing machine or treadmill with a computer program comparable to the NORAD command center. But the novelty soon wears off and several months later they are getting less benefit from the personal gym than they did from the second membership card since you can't carry a treadmill in your wallet. Guess what their next step is?

They lay out more money for new equipment which they think will be easier or less boring.

For guys who are always talking about having their money work for them, they have a hard time grasping the idea that spending more money for workouts isn't working out.

In contrast a lot of regular guys are usually too tired from working to work out. Other regular guys know more equipment isn't going to help. The rusty set of weights in the basement is enough evidence for them. Laying out more money isn't the answer. One dumbbell in the house is enough.

Some regular guys, especially the younger ones, do exercise. They play basketball, softball or football once a week, or swim at the YMCA. Others who exercise at home stick to sit-ups and push-ups because, "That's the way we did it in the Army."

Some of them actually do go out and run. But when they do, they don't make a spectacle of themselves. They wear old sweatpants, usually grey, and a sweatshirt with the logo of their favorite sports team. Regular guys don't wear Lycra clothing. It's too revealing, too revolting, too repulsive.

Besides, a baggy sweatsuit is a lot more practical. If you're out jogging in a skin-tight leotard and the cops drive by, where are you going to hide the beer can?

Keep on Truckin'

Regular guys like American cars and trucks. We like for them to run well and we like for them to run a long time.

We don't want one of those little cars with a lawnmower engine. We're a lot less interested in power seats, windows and antennas than we are in power under the hood. The fewer gizmos and gadgets on a car, the fewer things there are to go wrong.

Regular guys know how to change a tire, the oil, the filters, the plugs, and the head and tail lights. We know a feeler gauge isn't something you use to measure the softness of Corinthian leather.

We get more satisfaction in getting another 60,000 miles out of an old Chevy pickup truck than we would in picking up a new $60,000 car. We know the sticker price isn't the measure of the person who drives it.

Regular guys get a little tired of seeing low performance drivers in high performance cars. Part of it is that these young, trendy people took a real workman's automobile – the four-wheel-drive, all-purpose truck – and turned it into a yuppiemobile. You can tell when the owner isn't regular. He never gets that truck dirty. And he pays someone else to wash the dust off of it. That's because he doesn't want to ruin his manicure.

The question is, what does a guy like that need with a 4-wheel-drive truck? What does he need with any kind of truck? When was the last time he needed to move a half-ton load of conduit or a dozen rolls of barbed wire?

Does he think a truck will make him look more like a working man? He should know better. The hairdryer plugged into the cigarette lighter gives him away.

Arf Arf

A dog is about the most regular pet a guy could have.

When we were kids, we might have kept everything from hamsters to turtles. But our dogs were our *real* pets. And not just any dog will do. Regular guys don't want a full-grown dog that looks like a puppy. We want a real dog. One that's big enough to carry a pheasant or a duck. We don't want one that's small enough to carry in your pocket.

Regular guys want a good ol' dog, not one of those fancy, fluffy, yippie, yappy, yuppie dogs.

We don't want poodles. Poodles have hairdos. We want a dog that points, not primps.

Regular guys treat their dogs right. We don't put bows in a dog's hair or little antlers or bells on them at Christmas.

Regular guys talk to their dogs. But we don't talk baby talk. We often take our dogs along when we go hunting or fishing or just for a walk in the woods. That's because a regular dog is good company. A dog never complains about having to ride in the truck. He's happy just getting to go along. He'll even protect the truck while you're in the hardware store picking up some finishing nails.

A regular dog goes along with whatever you want to do. A dog is perfectly happy sitting in front of the TV all day or taking a ride in the country.

If you get excited about the game on TV, he gets excited right along with you. And you don't have to explain what happened. A regular dog knows when you're sad and will stay by your side without pestering you with questions.

A good ol' dog is always happy to see you, even when you come stumbling in at 2 A.M.

Pets That Aren't Regular

- Vietnamese potbellied pigs
- canaries, cockatoos, flamingos
- snakes, rattlers or otherwise
- fresh water parrot fish (at $150 a fish)
- ferrets, minks, or mongooses
- spider monkeys (or any other kind of monkey)

Regular Guys are Mallaphobic

Regular guys don't shop. We buy.

We don't go out looking for things to buy. We go out only when we can't put off buying a specific item.

Our favorite stores are the hardware store, the bait store, or the outdoors store. We also will go into the grocery store on occasion.

We don't go to stores that spell shop "Shoppe" or have "Boutique" in their names.

We prefer stores that have words like Mart, Discount, City, Warehouse, or Value in their names. K-Mart and Wal-Mart are prime examples. A store called Discount Value City is sure to be a winner.

A Down-Scale Guy in an Up-Scale Store (a horror story)

Lord, I hate to shop. What's this place? The Image Makers. I don't need to remake my image. But what the heck. Maybe I can give a new image as a gift.

Excuse me, Miss. Somebody's made a big mistake here. This just can't be right. Here's a game of tic-tac-toe, and it costs $20. My kids play it with pencil and paper for free.

Well, sir. Those Xs and Os are gold-plated, solid brass pieces.

Isn't that dangerous? My kids would get mad and crack each other's skulls open with heavy pieces like that.

Oh. This isn't for kids, Sir. It's an executive gift.

Executive gift? You mean these tycoons are sitting in their board rooms playing tic-tac-toe? No wonder the economy's in such bad shape. Do you have something a little more practical?

Well, here are some magnetic playing cards. See, it says here on the package that you can use them at the beach, on deck, or in bed because they are windproof.

It doesn't get windy in my bed. Except, of course, when the wife fixes bean soup. But we don't play cards in bed, or any of those other places for that matter. Besides, they're $27.50. That's 53 cents a card.

If price is the problem, here's something you might like. These little plastic balls filled with water. You freeze them and put them in drinks. That way you cool down your drinks with out watering them down. You get 24 of them for $6.

They wouldn't work for me. They're too big to fit through in the hole in the top of a beer can.

Maybe you would like to try our shave gel, after shave splash and after shave lotion. These three small containers are $47.95. We call it our face maintenance program.

Face maintenance? I'll bet you have trouble maintaining a straight face when you quote those prices. I could get a helluva lot of Aqua Velva after shave for that price.

Perhaps, Sir, this space pen would do. It writes at any angle, even upside down and underwater!

Look, Lady. I don't want to seem rude. But if I'm upside down and underwater, I don't think I'm going to start jotting down a grocery list. Know what I mean?

Oh, there's something I recognize. It's that plastic barf like they used to sell in joke shops.

No, Sir. That's a telephone. It's supposed to look like a slice of pizza.

All these gadgets and prices are making me a little nervous.

Well, then, Sir. We've got lots of things to help you relax. Here's a heavy-duty solar massager. You lay down, put it under your legs, and it shakes your entire body 150 times a minute. It's very popular among Japanese business executives. They use it for a mid-day break.

I don't think so. First of all, if my boss caught me lying down on the job, I would need a new job, not a massage. Secondly, if my body were shaken that much after lunch, I wouldn't need that plastic barf over there, either.

That's pizza, Sir.

Whatever.

Perhaps you'd like to try a rest shield.

Is that anything like my wife's dress shields? I don't need those. I used Right Guard anti-perspirant.

No, Sir. I already knew you used Right Guard. A rest shield is like a pair of glasses that shines either red, yellow or green light on your eyes. Red increases your energy, yellow makes you more creative, and green helps you relax. It's $150.

No thanks. I'll just watch the traffic lights. Besides, I would see red every time I remembered how much green I laid out for that contraption. I find it hard to believe that all these up-scale people fall for such tomfoolery. What's that thing over there?

That's one of our most popular new items.

What does it do?

Well, it has two motors that twirl a piece of string around in the air while a light shines on it. It doesn't have a real function. You see it's a....

Wait! Don't tell me. It's totally useless so it has to be an executive gift, right?

Yes, Sir. I guess you're not interested in that. Maybe you would like this fisherman's sweater. It's $129.95. It's made of imported wool and specially conceived by a New York designer.

Lady, I hate to tell you this, but you don't wear designer sweaters when you go fishing. First, it's white. You don't wear white—especially when you use live bait and clean your own fish. Secondly, it's $129.95. That's more than I paid for my Sunday suit.

Maybe your wife would like this electric jar opener. It unscrews tight lids off glass jars.

Maybe she would. But I don't dare risk it. I suspect that's the only reason she keeps me around.

What's this gadget here? It looks kind of like my power screwdriver without the blade.

No, that's the thermometer of the future to take your temperature.

It's too short to reach under your tongue. What do you do with it?

Stick it in your ear.

Look sister, you don't have to get rude. Stick it in your own ear—I'm out of here. I've never seen a place that had so many things that nobody needs.

Food

"Great. Now what have you got to eat."

Chowin' Down

Regular guys like food we can sink our teeth into. We want a main course that covers the plate. We don't like lunch to be something on a bed of lettuce.

We like plain food, not something stuffed into flower blossoms. We have to be able to pronounce it and recognize it on sight before we'll eat it. We want our vegetables to be grownups. We don't like cold soup or hot salad.

We do like potato salad. In fact we like potatoes just about anyway we get them – French-fried, home fried, baked, twice-baked, scalloped, and mashed. We like potatoes in hash and hash-browned.

We like potato chips, potato pancakes and potato soup. We like potatoes covered with melted cheese and bacon, or sour cream and chives. But most of all we like them covered with gravy.

Other regular guy staples are beef, peanut butter, and bread. We like cold cuts and hot dogs. We want our chicken country-fried, not skinless and baked or wrapped in some kind of leaves.

Regular guys like party snacks by the handful, not on toothpicks. Pass the popcorn, peanuts, and Chex party mix, if you please.

We like bacon and eggs for breakfast, hamburgers and fries for lunch, and meatloaf and potatoes for dinner.

Steak is a favorite, special-occasion food. Regular guys like to cook them on a charcoal grill or order them at a restaurant. Whether it's a T-bone, rib eye, New York strip, or Porterhouse cooked rare, medium, or medium-rare, regular guys will eat it. We will eat steak just about any way but raw.

To a regular guy, steak tartare is bunch of ca-ca.

Regular Foods, A to Z

A*pple pie, apple butter, apple cider, apples*
B*ologna, baked beans, bratwurst, biscuits, bacon, bread*
C*atfish, chili, Cheez Whiz, cabbage, corn flakes*
D*onuts, deviled eggs, dumplings, Dinty Moore Stew*
E*ggs, elk, enchiladas*
F*rench fries, fried chicken, flapjacks, fish, Fig Newton cookies*
G*ravy, garlic bread, green tomatoes (fried), gingerbread*
H*am, hamburgers, hot dogs, hash, hushpuppies*
I*ce Cream, Italian meatballs*
J*elly, jerky, Jell-o gelatin, jam*
K*abobs (beef), kosher dill pickles*
L*iver & onions, lasagna, leftovers*
M*eat loaf, mashed potatoes, macaroni & cheese, milkshakes*
N*oodles, nachos, New England clam chowder*
O*nion rings, oatmeal cookies, orange juice*
P*ot roast, peanut butter, pork chops, pizza, pumpkin pie*
Q*uarter pounder with cheese, quail, quantity, Quik drink mix*
R*oast beef, ravioli, rabbit, rolls, rye bread*
S*teak, sausage, spaghetti, salami, stew, Sloppy Joes*
T*rout, tabasco, tenderloin, turkey, tuna-noodle casserole*
U*pside-down cake*
V*eal parmesan, vegetable soup, venison, vanilla milkshakes*
W*atermelon, waffles, western omelettes*
X*-tra servings*
Y*ams, yeast rolls*
Z*ucchini (fried)*

He Wouldn't Touch That with a 10-Foot Fork

***A**lfalfa sprouts, anchovies, asparagus tips, aspic, avocados*
***B**amboo shoots, bean sprouts, brussels sprouts, blossoms*
***C**anapés, caviar, cottage cheese, cucumber mousse*
***D**uck à l'orange, dolphin*
***E**ggplant, endive, escargot, eggs benedict*
***F**oie gras, fondue, fugu**
***G**azpacho, guacamole, guava*
***H**erb tea, hors d'oeuvres*
***I**nstant soup, instant breakfast, instant coffee*
***J**ello salad (especially the kind with carrots and cabbage)*
***K**elp, kidney pie, kumquats*
***L**eeks, lettuce soup, lobster newburg, lotus root salad*
***M**angos, meringue surprise, marzipan*
***N**ouvelle anything*
***O**at bran, octopus*
***P**âté, parsley, papaya, parsnips, poached anything, prunes*
***Q**uiche, quail eggs*
***R**addichio, rhubarb-raspberry cream bombe*
***S**oufflés, sushi, squid, steak tartare, sukiyaki*
***T**ofu, turkey hamburger, turnips*
***U**rchins*
***V**ichyssoise*
***W**atercress, wilted lettuce salad*
***X** any food that begins with X shouldn't be trusted*
***Y**ogurt*
***Z**ucchini (steamed)*

* poisonous Japansese blow fish

When the Dishes are Dirty...

Regular guys go out to eat. They don't go out to dine. They aren't interested in paying extra for ambiance. Ambiance doesn't stick to your ribs.

The regular guy's restaurant offers plenty of good food at a good price. He's satisfied if he sits down to a full plate and stands up with a full stomach. He's happier with burgers and shakes or pizza and beer than with appetizers and entrées.

That's why hamburger stands, steak houses, and diners are more his fare than five-star restaurants. If he's going out to a nice place for a special occasion, he's going to pick a nice, friendly place.

Here are some tips for telling whether a restaurant is regular.

If there is valet parking and a large canopy over the front sidewalk, it's not regular. But it is regular if there's a 20-foot-tall pirate, chicken, clown, cowboy, or big fat guy out front.

It's regular if the name of the restaurant has the following words:

– burgers, chicken, tacos, pizza, spaghetti, or pancakes
– home cooking, country, or family-style
– western, Amish, Dutch, or diner

A sign proclaiming "Bar-Bee-Q" is another regular tip-off.

Words that hint a restaurant is not regular include:

– cuisine, nouvelle, and vegetarian
– Hungarian, Indian, and Japanese

If the restaurant has the owner's first name like Hank's or Tony's or Mary's, it's probably regular. If the restaurant has someone's last name that sounds foreign, like Sardi's, it's probably not. McDonald's is an exception, of course.

If the name of the restaurant begins with "La" or ends in "aux," it's definitely not regular.

If the place advertises fish instead of seafood, it's regular. If it has coupons in the newspaper or advertises a once-a-week special of "all you can eat for $4.95," it's regular.

If it serves Sunday brunch, it's not regular. If it serves breakfast 24-hours a day, it is.

If there's a neon sign in the window saying "steaks and chops" or "shakes & fries," it's regular.

If there is a notice of "reservations only," it's not regular. If there's a sign saying "truckers welcome," it is.

If you can see all the seats from the door, it's regular. If there are all stools at a counter, it's real regular.

If there are velvet ropes on brass poles to control the crowd, it's not regular. If there are plastic chains on stainless steel poles, it is.

If it has padded arm chairs, it's not regular. If it has highchairs and booster seats, it is.

If there are plastic flowers on the table, it's regular. If there are candles, it's not.

If you get more than two forks, it's not regular.

If you are offered coffee right off the bat, it is.

If they bring finger bowls instead of those little wet towelettes, it's not regular. If it takes more than two people to greet you, seat you and serve you, it's not regular.

If you can't get the waiter's attention, it's not regular. If you can get your own soup and salad, it is.

If the waiter pours a taste of wine for your approval, it's not regular. If he sets a pitcher of beer on the table, it is.

If you watch them cook the food on a grill behind the counter, it's regular. If you watch them cook it at your table, it's not.

If there's a dessert cart, it's probably not regular. If you are too full for dessert, it probably is.

If they hand you the check in a little booklet, it's not regular. If the waitress calls off the items and adds up the tab in front of you, it is.

If you pay at the cash register, it's regular. If you pay through the nose, it's not.

Entertainment

PETE'S
BAR & GRILL

That's Entertainment

Regular guys just want to have fun. And we don't need to spend a fortune to have it.

We have fun discussing the pre-season polls with our buddies down at the neighborhood tavern or playing a game of Chutes and Ladders with the kids.

The shows we like to watch don't require opera glasses or pricey tickets. A remote is all we need.

We like to relax with books, magazines, and music, as long as the stories, articles, and songs are about regular things like trucks, jobs and dogs that are more faithful than the gal who slipped away.

Here's to You, Pal

The regular guy appreciates an occasional good shot of Wild Turkey whiskey almost as much as he appreciates a clear shot at one.

When a regular guy drinks, he drinks like a man. Beer is his first preference. American beer. Blue Ribbon is a blue collar, regular brand of beer. So are Budweiser, Iron City and Schlitz. No imported malt is worth the dough.

He also likes whiskey. Sometimes he drinks beer and whiskey together and calls it a boilermaker. A drink couldn't have a more regular name.

He doesn't drink anything frozen, frothy, or sweet. A Long Island Iced isn't his cup of tea. He doesn't drink martinis. They cost too much and the olive or onion takes up too much room in the glass.

Today's guy doesn't drink and drive. He has plenty of friends who will give him a lift if he ever needs it.

Things Found in a Regular Bar

1. knotty pine
2. a jukebox with at least one Willie Nelson song on it
3. a bartender who knows your nickname
4. a jar of deviled eggs or pickled pigs' knuckles
5. a TV for sports
6. a softball team at the bar
7. a couple of softball team trophies behind the bar
8. a card game in the corner or back room
9. a pool table or dart board
10. a spittoon
11. paper napkins with jokes on them

Things Not Found in Regular Bars

1. ferns
2. Muzak
3. a bartender who wears a tie and calls you "sir"
4. dainty sandwiches and hors d'oeuvres on toothpicks
5. a karaoke machine
6. a cover charge
7. a wine list
8. downsized beer glasses
9. a jazz trio
10. clean restrooms

Horray for Hollywood

Siskel and Ebert aren't regular guys. They have to see a movie before knowing whether they like it or not. Regular guys know what they like, and that's all they go to see.

They like everything from westerns to crime to comedy as long as it's regular. To be a regular movie it has to have plenty of action, a little cleavage, and the good guys have to win.

Robin Hood met the criteria. *Little Man Tate* did not.

Regular guys like movies with submarines but not with subtitles. They like movies with Henry Fonda. But they aren't fonda Jane. They like *Mr. Robert* but not *Mr. Mom.* They loved the *African Queen* and hated *The King and I.* Stopping the action every five minutes to sing and dance isn't regular.

They prefer movies in which the boys are going to war instead of coming of age.

Some actors, like John Wayne, they like in all movies. Others, like Alan Alda, they don't like in any movie.

Some guys they like in some movies but not in others. For example they watched Robert Redford in *Butch Cassidy and the Sundance Kid* but not in *The Way We Were.* Regular guys weren't that way.

They like sports-related movies, such as *Field of Dreams, North Dallas Forty, The Longest Yard, The Natural, Bull Durham,* and *Major League.* They like boxing movies such as *Rocky,* but not films like *Karate Kid III.* Regular guys don't fight with their feet.

Here are some other movies regular guys would watch on TV or the VCR:

1. *Ben Hur*
2. *Crocodile Dundee*
3. *Fort Apache* (not the Bronx)
4. *The Good, the Bad, and the Ugly*
5. *The Godfather*
6. *Hang 'Em High*
7. *The Maltese Falcon*
8. *The Shootist*
9. *Shane*
10. *Smokey and the Bandit*
11. *The Magnificent 7* (they particularly like the theme song)

One last note on movies. It's about the movie regular guys resent the most. One of those male-bashing flicks like *Thelma and Louise,* you may think.

No sir. It's *Bambi*.

Up until Walt Disney made those forest critters talk like people, this country respected a guy who could go into the woods with a gun and put meat on the table for his family. Bambi, Thumper, and Flower changed all that. Now a guy can't even put on a camouflage cap without someone pointing an accusing finger and spitting out, "Bambi killer!"

Why couldn't he have made that cartoon about a chicken? Regular guys could live without that.

Regular Guys in the Movies

1. John Wayne
2. John Wayne
3. John Wayne
4. Sylvester Stallone
5. Steve McQueen
6. Paul Newman
7. James Coburn
8. James Garner
9. Burt Reynolds
10. Henry Fonda
11. Jack Palance
12. Charlton Heston
14. Yosemite Sam, you varmint!
15. Humphrey Bogart
16. Clint Eastwood

Cut!

Regular guys stay away from movies starring:

1. Alan Alda
2. Woody Allen
3. Michael J. Fox
4. Pee-Wee Herman
5. Martin Short
6. Ryan O'Neal
7. Patrick Swayze
8. Richard Burton
9. Dustin Hoffman
10. Rick Moranis

Regular Guy Reading

Who says you can't judge a book by its cover? The regular guy can tell what he likes and what he doesn't with just a glance at the title or back of the jacket.

He's always had his favorite authors—Jack London, Hemingway, Mark Twain, and Tom Clancy are regular fare. And if he strays from fiction for awhile, there are plenty of biographies about coaches and players. A lot of them are written by newspaper sports columnists, so he hasn't strayed too far from fiction.

But turn the regular guy loose in the mall bookstore for 10 minutes while he's waiting for his wife (who's returning the potholders he gave her for her birthday), and you get an idea of how a regular guy edits his book choices....

Damn. Look at all those books. I can't believe there are that many people who know something important enough to write down. Let's see what's on this best sellers table.

Hmmm, *I Remember* by Dan Rather. I'd rather remember Walter. Uh oh. One of those men's movement poetry books—*Fire in the Belly* by Sam Keem. If he thinks he's got fire in the belly now, he should try some of my chili.

Lighten Up, George by Art Buchwald. This oughta be good. Anybody that pokes fun at politicians is all right in my book.

Selling the Dream by some guy called Guy Kawasaki. The Japanese have been buying up the American dream for about 10 years. Now he wants to turn around and sell it back.

Shirley MacLaine has another one out. *Dance While You Can.* According to her other books, she's already danced her way through a few centuries.

Ah ha! Here's one *Rules of Engagement* by Joe Weber. It's got a fighter plane on the front so it's probably not a pre-wedding etiquette book. Looks kinda' good. A real regular book.

Here's one about old Winnie. *Churchill, a Life.* Good lord, it's got 1066 pages. It's almost as fat as he was. Wait a minute, wasn't 1066 the Battle of Hastings?

What's this *Fates Worse than Death* about? Hmmm. Kurt Vonnegut gives us an autobiographical collage of the 1980's. Give us a break, Kurt. Regular guys are trying to forget the '80s.

Oh, here's something. *You Gotta Play Hurt.* That sounds interesting. Hey, it's by Dan Jenkins. He wrote *Semi-Tough,* which wasn't half bad.

Ha! *You Just Don't Understand—Women and Men in Conversation,* by Deborah Tannen. Of course I won't understand. My wife has to tell me everything five times before I get it.

Oh, great. Just what we needed—another book about Madonna. *Madonna Unauthorized,* another behind-the-scenes look at her. Haven't we seen enough of her behind? Whoa! What's this? *How To Stay Alive in the Woods.* Anybody that needs this just ought to stay out of the woods.

"No thanks, Miss. I'm just browsing. I get all my books free at the library. But do you mind if I ask a personal question? Would *you* be upset if a guy gave you potholders for your birthday?"

A Regular Guy's Reading List

Things He Reads

- price tags
- score boards
- the thermometer
- directions
- *The Night Before Christmas*
- voltage meter
- half the memos from his boss
- kids' report cards
- tire pressure gauges
- whatever's in the bathroom

Things He Doesn't Read

- tea leaves
- his wife's mind
- recipes
- TV listings (that's what remotes are for)
- junk mail
- leaflets from weirdos on the street
- half the memos from his boss
- safety warnings on spray paint cans
- ingredients and calorie labels
- George Bush's lips

Slick Reading

Give regular guys credit. Ammo clips aren't the only magazines a regular guy buys.

He even likes the popular titles, like *Popular Mechanics* and *Popular Science*. He'll read *People* magazine if his wife leaves it in the bathroom, but he's not the sort of man who reads *Playboy*; he just looks at the pictures. He mostly sticks to the magazines that are written for guys who like and do regular things. His magazines have words like sports, outdoors, and cars in them.

Sports Illustrated is a good illustration of this. He looks forward to reading it even when it's not the swimsuit edition.

He'll read general news magazines and will thumb through a copy of *Life* for old time's sake at the newsstand, but he doesn't read *National Geographic*, even the 200 copies he has bundled up down in the basement.

He stays away from magazines that only have initials for names, *GQ* and *M* for example. He also shies away from *PC*, *PC World* and *PC Home*. Regular guys still believe that computers are anything but personal.

Some Regular Magazines

1. *Sports Illustrated*
2. *Outdoor Life*
3. *Sports Afield*
4. *American Angler*
5. *Road and Track*
6. *Hot Rod*
7. *Car and Driver*
8. *Consumer Reports*
9. *Family Handyman*
10. *Woodwork*

Some Not So Regular Magazines

1. *Vegetarian Times*
2. *Decanter*
3. *Bird Talk* (dedicated to better care for pet birds)
4. *Golf Digest*
5. *Yachting Monthly*
6. *Smithsonian*
7. *Runners World*
8. *Esquire*
9. *Entrepreneur*
10. *Gourmet*

Music to His Ears

The regular guy has a song in his heart. But if he had to sing for his supper, he'd starve.

He loves music and usually sticks with the type he grew up with—whether country, swing, jazz, or rock.

Regular guys generally appreciate the singers who have stood the test of time. Their recordings have outlasted most of the others of the same era—Ray Charles, James Taylor, Hank Williams, Sr., and Smokey Robinson are a few good examples.

Boy George, the Sex Pistols, and Ozzy Osbourne are not.

You don't have to unwrap the cellophane from the cassette tape to know that some groups aren't regular. Their names give them away. For instance, you can bet your Johnny Paycheck collection that a group called "Membranes" isn't regular. Neither are Teenage Jesus and the Jerks, Stinky Toys, or Virgin Prunes.

No thanks. We'll stick with Bruce Springsteen, Neil Diamond, John Mellencamp, and, of course, Elvis. We'll just listen. We won't try to sing along. Regular guys usually don't know the words.

Song Lyrics the Regular Guy Does Know

1. "The Star-Spangled Banner"
2. "One Hundred Bottles of Beer on the Wall"
3. "Jingle Bells"
4. "Take Me Out to the Ball Game"
5. "Happy Birthday"
6. "Row, Row, Row Your Boat"
7. "Home on the Range"
8. "Rudolph the Red-Nosed Reindeer"
9. "Yankee Doodle"
10. "Charge!" (The bugle call played at ball games—Ta-da-da-dat ta-da—"Charge!")

Games Regular Guys Play

Regular guys putter around the house. We don't putt into a cup that automatically returns the ball back across the livingroom floor.

Regular guys like to play poker and euchre with the boys, and board games with the kids. A lot of us play rotisserie baseball—a game based on the averages of individual professional players. It keeps us interested in the season, even when our team's chances for the pennant are down the tubes.

At home we play checkers, not chess; Parcheesi instead of Monopoly; and gin rummy instead of Trivial Pursuit.

The regular guy usually doesn't have the patience for a jigsaw puzzle unless it's one he gave to the kids with a sports picture on it.

We like Yahtzee because it's something like poker with dice. We like the game Battleship as long as it's the original and not the electronic version. And we don't want anything to do with video games. Pinball machines are about as high-tech as a game should be.

We play Chutes and Ladders with the kids, and we're not sorry for any of the times we've played Sorry. A regular guy will cheat on occasion to let a tyke win.

In a game of Scrabble, we don't let our wives or girlfriends win. The women do it on their own.

Clue is not a mystery to us. We play dominos instead of backgammon. We like the kids' Mr. Mouth. We pretend we're flipping flies into the yawning mouth of the office bore.

The regular guy also likes carnival games at the fair. He knows the odds are stacked against him. But that doesn't stop him from trying to knock over milk bottles, burst balloons, or wham the lever with a mallet to flip rubber frogs onto a floating lily pad.

It's really fun. Why else would a regular guy walk around all day, proudly clutching a pink, fuzzy teddy bear under his arm?

Regular Times

January
Sun Mon Tues Wed Thur Fri Sat
Bowl Games 1-9PM
More Bowl Games
P.U. Beer for Super Bowl
Car show at Armory
Pro Bowl
Super Bowl
February
Wed Thur Fri
Lincoln's B'day
days to Superbowl
June
Sun Mon Tues Wed Thur Fri Sat
Softball practice
Camping trip with Bonnie's Scout Troop
Little League Ump.
Opening softball game
Softball
Class reunion
Flag Day
Boat Show Armory
July
Tues Wed Thur Fri
P.U. Suzie's parade dress @ cleaners
P.U. 6pack for Simpsons
Softball night game
October
Sun Mon Tues Wed Thur Fri Sat
Playoffs begin
Hunting season opens
P.U. Beer for series
World Series
Suzie's B'day
Halloween
Ref basketball
Start to make Halloween costumes
Sun Mon
62 days to Super Bowl

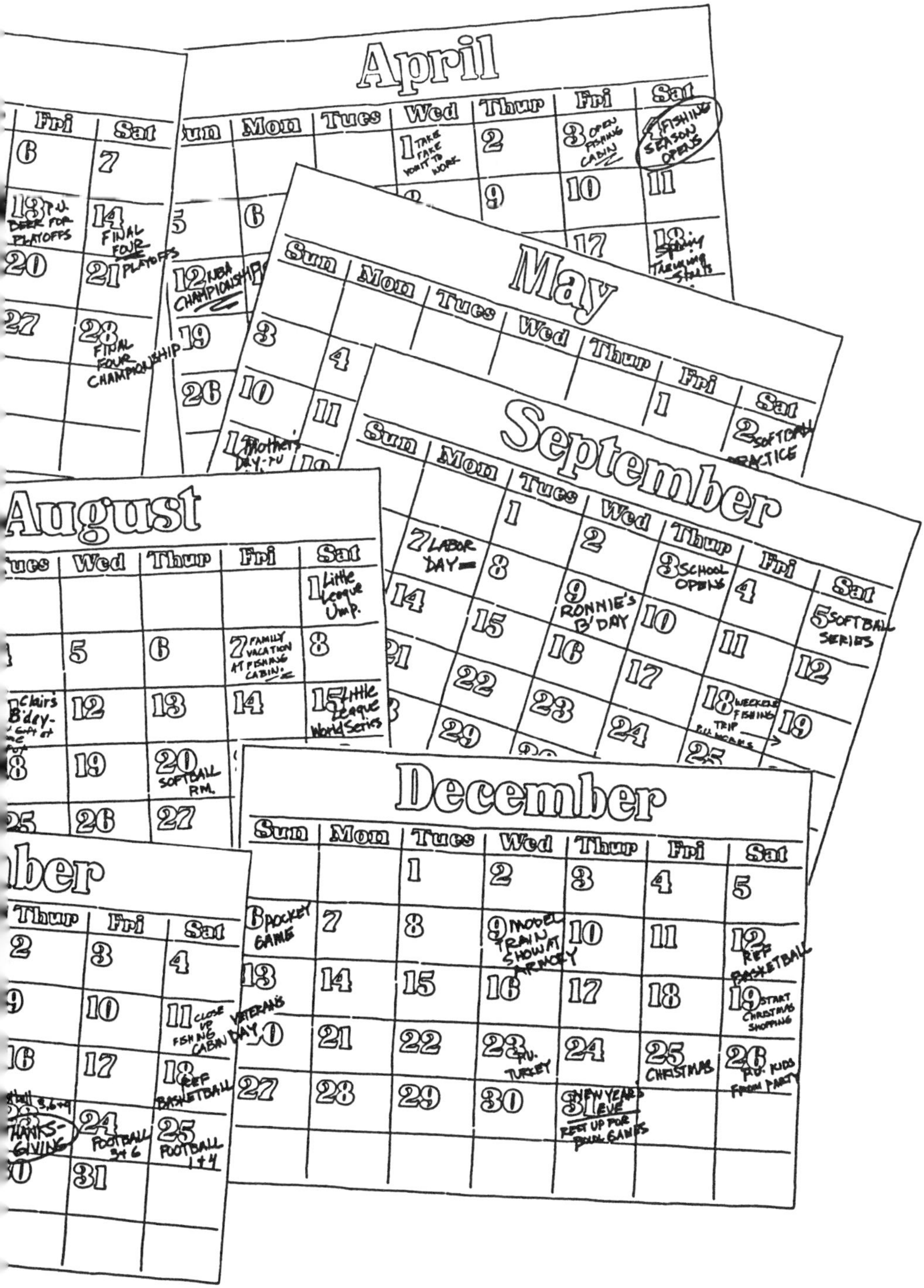
April
Sun Mon Tues Wed Thur Fri Sat
1 TAKE FAKE VOMIT TO WORK
3 OPEN FISHING CABIN
4 FISHING SEASON OPENS
12 NBA CHAMPIONSHIP
13 P.U. BEER FOR PLAYOFFS
14 FINAL FOUR PLAYOFFS
28 FINAL FOUR CHAMPIONSHIP
May
Sun Mon Tues Wed Thur Fri Sat
17 Mother's Day-P.U.
September
Sun Mon Tues Wed Thur Fri Sat
2 SOFTBALL PRACTICE
3 SCHOOL OPENS
5 SOFTBALL SERIES
7 LABOR DAY
9 RONNIE'S B'DAY
18 WEEKEND FISHING TRIP
August
Tues Wed Thur Fri Sat
1 Little League Ump.
7 FAMILY VACATION AT FISHING CABIN
11 Clair's B'day-
15 Little League World Series
20 SOFTBALL PM.
December
Sun Mon Tues Wed Thur Fri Sat
6 HOCKEY GAME
9 MODEL TRAIN SHOW AT ARMORY
12 REF BASKETBALL
19 START CHRISTMAS SHOPPING
23 P.U. TURKEY
25 CHRISTMAS
26 P.U. KIDS FROM PARTY
31 NEW YEAR'S EVE
REST UP FOR BOWL GAMES
mber
Thur Fri Sat
11 CLOSE UP FISHING CABIN
VETERAN'S DAY
18 REF BASKETBALL
THANKS-GIVING
24 FOOTBALL 3+6
25 FOOTBALL 1+4

Regular Times

The regular guy may have paint on his hands. He may have grease on his hands. He's probably got a few nicks and cuts on his hands.

But one thing he doesn't have on his hands is time.

He uses his free time to do regular things like fishing and working around the house. He enjoys his vacation time in regular vacation places.

He has his favorite times of year and his favorite holiday times.

Some times are more regular than others. For instance, the opening day of hunting season is a lot more regular than Valentine's Day.

He keeps track of all these times on a calendar. Not just any calendar. A *regular* calendar.

Let's thumb through it. We might just have a good time.

Daze of the Month Regular Guy Calendars

1. The 365-Sports-Facts-a-Year-Calendar
2. The 1992 Dave Barry Calendar
3. The Michael Jordan 16-Month Calendar
4. The Gardener's Calendar
5. The Sports Illustrated Swimsuit Calendar
6. Classy Cars Calendar
7. The Dogs Calendar
8. Norman Rockwell Calendar
9. The 1992 Weather Guide Calendar
10. The Trains Calendar
11. The Farmer's Almanac

Thanks, But No Thanks

1. Llewellyn's Astrological Calendar
2. Cathy's Life, Liberty & the Pursuit of Youth Calendar
3. William F. Buckley Jr.'s 366-Words-You'd-Like-to-Know Calendar
4. The Lamborghini Calendar
5. C * A * T * S Calendar
6. The Baby Animals Calendar
7. The Calendar of Inspirational Poems and Prayers
8. The Van Gogh Calendar
9. New Kids on the Block Calendar
10. The Art Institute of Chicago Monet Calendar
11. The Far Side Wiener Dog Art Calendar

Away From It All

When the regular guy has free time, a weekend, or vacation, he is likely to head for the hills, the lakes or the woods. Or he may knock around the house, putter around the yard or run around with the kids. He won't play a round of golf.

On weekends the regular guy doesn't feel whole unless he starts a project around the house, does some yard work, watches a ball game, does something with the kids, and has a family dinner that, if possible, includes parents or other family.

A lot of regular guys like to go hunting, fishing, or camping. Some like to shoot ducks. Some like to shoot deer. Some like to shoot pool, and some just like to shoot the bull with the guy next door.

A regular guy goes camping just to get away from it all. He doesn't go in an RV with a TV, a CD, or a PC. That's not getting away from it all. That's taking it all along. A tent and canoe are more his style.

The regular guy doesn't "winter in Cancun" or "summer in Nantucket." He does know some limericks about Nantucket, but he doesn't go there. He is more apt to be at a cottage or cabin on some small lake or stream.

You won't find a regular guy on nude beaches at St. Thomas or in Speedo swimming suits anywhere. He doesn't go to golf, tennis, or health resorts. He stays away from dude ranches and fat farms.

He will take his family to zoos and aquariums. He may even go to theme parks like Sea World and Disney World. But he stays at the Motel 6 or Days Inn motel a few miles away instead of the resort hotels on the grounds.

Traveling on vacation makes a regular guy appreciate home a little more. He says it's kind of like hitting yourself on the head with a hammer because it feels so good when you stop.

Things a Regular Guy Thinks He Would Do If He Had More Time

1. go fishing
2. go hunting
3. build something–either big like a cabin, or fancy like a gun cabinet
4. restore a '56 Chevy
5. load his own shotgun shells or tie his own fishing flies
6. sort through his old *Field and Stream* magazines
7. go back home and look up his old high school coach
8. get in touch with his old army buddies
9. teach his kids something really important, like how to lay concrete block
10. set up the old Lionel trains

Things a Regular Guy Really Does When He Has Extra Time

1. goes fishing
2. goes hunting
3. puts up shelves in the basement
4. changes the oil in the truck
5. goes on a Boy Scout camp-out
6. cleans the gutters
7. cleans the gutters for the widow across the street
8. gives the dog a flea bath
9. works on a Lion's Club fund drive
10. takes a nap

A Regular Guy's Favorite Season

Autumn is the regular guy's favorite time of the year because:

1. fall is three seasons rolled into one – football season, baseball season, and hunting season
2. he can quit mowing the grass
3. he can start wearing his plaid flannel shirt again
4. fall foliage, apple cider, and pumpkin pie
5. the L.L. Bean Christmas Catalog arrives
6. new episodes of *Cheers* and *Coach* are on TV
7. Thanksgiving is coming
8. no more zucchini and tomatoes from the neighbors
9. the smell of gunpowder is in the woods
10. chain saws and attic insulation are on sale

The Regular Guy's Favorite Day

Thanksgiving day wins, hands down. It comes in the Fall, the regular guy's most favorite time of year. It is a true American holiday, and it doesn't require him to shop for a gift for his wife. It's always on Thursday, which usually means the start of a four-day weekend.

Ten Things Regular Guys Like About Thanksgiving

1. mashed potatoes and gravy
2. football at noon*
3. turkey
4. football at 3 P.M.
5. sweet potatoes and marshmallows
6. football at 6 P.M.
7. bread dressing and gravy
8. football at 9 P.M.
9. pumpkin pie and whipped cream
10. he can do it all again on Friday

* West Coast guys can get an early start with football at 9 A.M.

Holidays and Thoughts

New Year's Eve – I'm not going to any party where they wear silly hats and blow those stupid horns. Besides there are too many amateur drunks out there. We pros stay home.

New Year's Day – Glad I stayed home last night. Nothing worse than having a hangover when you're trying to watch a dozen bowl games.

Groundhog Day – I don't care what month it is. If you see a groundhog stick his head out of the ground, shoot the varmint! The same goes for TV weathermen. They aren't any more accurate than groundhogs.

St. Valentine's Day – Regular guys ought to work to get this day abolished. Somehow we usually end up in trouble with our wives or girlfriends over this.

President's Day – Ain't that just like Congress? Taking away Washington's and Lincoln's birthdays and giving us a President's Day on nobody's birthday. Washington and Lincoln would have vetoed that one.

St. Patrick's Day – Everybody is wearing green today, and a lot of folks will still be looking green tomorrow.

April Fools' Day – I swear those guys down at the plant aren't going to get me again this year.

Mother's Day – I won't forget to send a card. I won't forget to send a card. I won't forget to send a card. I won't forget to send a card. I won't forget to send a card.

Memorial Day – People ought to pay a little more attention to the meaning, and worry a little less about picnics, golf, and looking good in their bathing suits.

Flag Day – Every day is Flag Day at our house.

Father's Day – I hope they just let me go fishing.

Independence Day – I love it. Hot dogs, beer, baseball, American flags, fireworks, parades. Eat your heart out, England.

Labor Day – What they ought to do is make those congressmen, politicians, lawyers, judges, and pinstripe-suit-types do a *real* job for the day so they know what the working guy is up against.

"Now isn't that better than some silly ballerina costume?"

Columbus Day – I don't care what anybody says. He deserves some credit for making that journey. Hell, they didn't even have Coleman coolers to take along.

Halloween – "A turtle? Nah, you don't want to be a turtle, son. Here's what we'll do. We'll get some boxes and foil and build you a robot suit with flashing lights, and switches, and buttons. Oh, all right. Quit your sniffling. Be a turtle. Go get your mom to help."

Veterans' Day – These guys deserve a lot more than just a day.

Thanksgiving – Football, food, and fall. What more could a guy ask for?

Christmas – I think I'll get her a new fire extinguisher for the kitchen. She ought to like that.

Chestnuts Roasting

May it ever be so corny, there's no place like home for the holidays for the regular guy.

The regular guy doesn't go to Vail to ski, Cancun to sun, or Vegas to gamble over the holidays. He's home with family. If it's cold or snowy, he takes the kids sledding or ice skating and then back to the house for hot chocolate with marshmallows.

The secret wish of a lot of regular guys is to have an old-fashioned, relaxed, white Christmas in a rural area like Vermont or Montana with a fireplace, happy children, and sleighs pulled by horses from the beer commercials.

He's a traditionalist. He wants his wife and kids to bake and decorate cookies or string popcorn and cranberries while he puts up the tree, strings the lights, and hooks up the electric train around the base. He wants the whole family to join in the decorating while Bing Crosby croons *White Christmas* on the radio.

The regular guy's Christmas tree comes from a cut-your-own farm, not a box in the basement. The tree is lighted with strings of bulbs, not a flood light that changes from pink to blue to lavender as it reflects off the aluminum branches.

A lot of regular guys try to build something for their kids—a doll house, toy box, or playhouse—either from scratch or from a store-bought kit. He tries it at least once—and usually only once.

The regular guy typically volunteers with charity projects for the poor at Christmas time. He donates to traditional groups like the Salvation Army. He wants to share good times with relatives. He wants stores to quit rushing the holidays by setting up Christmas displays on Labor Day. But most of all, he wants his wife to do all the shopping.

Gifts a Regular Guy Appreciates

1. Craftsman power screwdriver
2. Fruit of the Loom underwear
3. fishing lures
4. nuts and candy gift box
5. sausage and cheese gift box
6. Aqua Velva after shave
7. sports bloopers and great moments video tapes
8. *Sports Illustrated* subscription
9. Coleman lantern
10. sipping whiskey, preferably Canadian Mist

A Regular Guy's Wife Sings About Christmas Over The Years

On our first year of Christmas, the big lug gave to me, a new Sears DieHard battery.

On our second year of Christmas, the big lug gave to me, two latex gloves and a new Sears DieHard battery.

On our third year of Christmas, the big lug gave to me, three trash cans, two latex gloves, and a new Sears DieHard battery.

On our fourth year of Christmas, the big lug gave to me, four carving knives, three trash cans, two latex gloves, and a new Sears DieHard battery.

On our fifth year of Christmas, the big lug gave to me, an alarm clock that **rings**; *four carving knives, three trash cans, two latex gloves, and a new Sears DieHard battery.*

On our sixth year of Christmas, the big lug gave to me, a book on fish fileting, an alarm clock that **rings**; *four carving knives, three trash cans, two latex gloves, and a new Sears DieHard battery.*

On our seventh year of Christmas, the big lug gave to me, clippers for toenail trimming, a book on fish fileting, an alarm clock that **rings**; *four carving knives, three trash cans, two latex gloves, and a new Sears DieHard battery.*

On our eighth year of Christmas, the big lug gave to me, eight homemade bookends, clippers for toenail trimming, a book on fish fileting, an alarm clock that **rings**; *four carving knives, three trash cans, two latex gloves, and a new Sears DieHard battery.*

On our ninth year of Christmas, the big lug gave to me, nine ladies hankies, eight homemade bookends, clippers for toenail trimming, a book on fish fileting, an alarm clock that **rings**; *four carving knives, three trash cans, two latex gloves, and a new Sears DieHard battery.*

On the tenth year of Christmas, the big lug gave to me, ten-foot jumper cables, nine ladies hankies, eight homemade bookends, clippers for toe nail trimming, a book on fish fileting, an alarm clock that **rings**; *four carving knives, three trash cans, two latex gloves, and a new Sears DieHard battery.*

On the eleventh year of Christmas, the big lug gave to me, 11 pints of perfume, ten-foot jumper cables, nine ladies hankies, eight homemade bookends, clippers for toenail trimming, a book on fish fileting, an alarm clock that **rings**; *four carving knives, three trash cans, two latex gloves, and a new Sears DieHard battery.*

On our twelfth year of Christmas, I bought a clock radio, wrapped it for myself, put it under the tree, told him not to worry, it's the thought that counts, Christmas is for kids, I'm happy with what I have, except for that clock that **rings**; *put that damn thing in a trash can, and please don't ever buy a gift for me ever again.*

Final

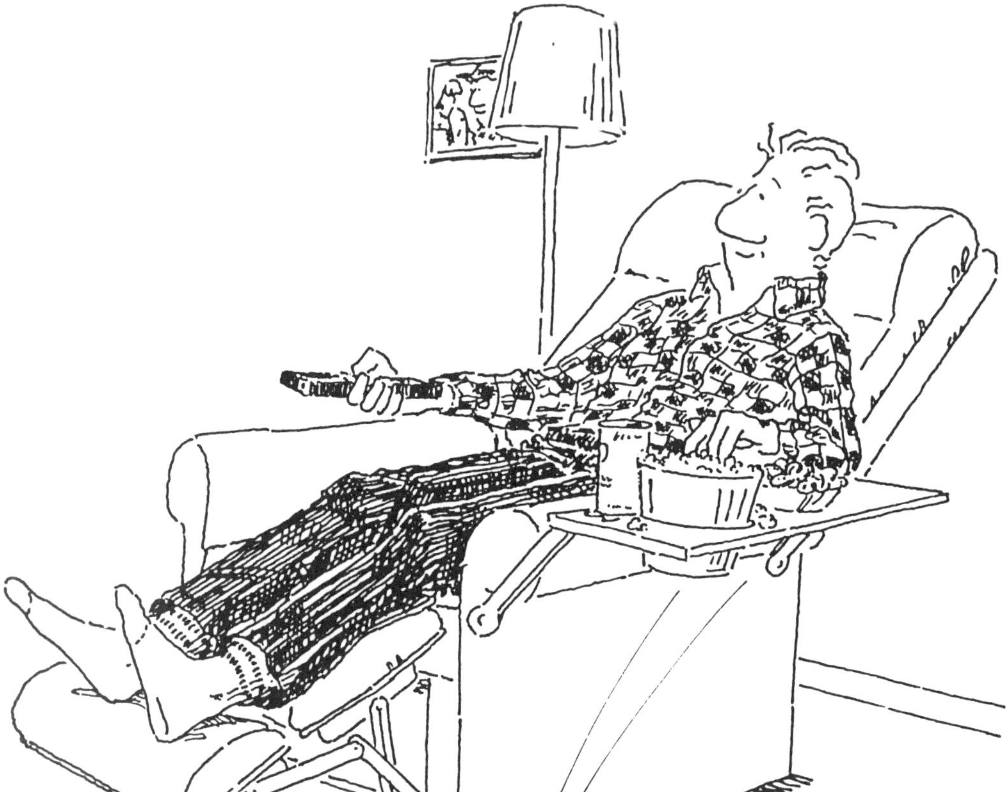

One Last Chance

Well, here we are. We've got this regular guy thing just about wrapped up tighter than a drum.

You've read all about being a regular guy, taken a couple of tests, and had a few laughs.

But it's come down to the wire. If you haven't already made up your mind, it's time to decide: Are you or are you not a regular guy?

Here's one more quiz to see if you've learned anything along the way. And just for good measure, there's a list of clues to help you spot some irregularities in yourself. Give it your best shot. We're pulling for ya, pal.

A Few Questions More

1. The first things I read in the paper are
   a. stock reports, society news, fashion columns
   b. Dear Abby, Ann Landers, Dr. Ruth
   c. sports section, comics, Dave Barry, Mike Royko

2. I have leather
   a. pants
   b. upholstery in the car
   c. work boots

3. In the fall, I
   a. hire a lawn service to vacuum the leaves
   b. use a blower to push them into my neighbor's yard
   c. tell the kids to rake them

4. "I've been working on the _______"
   a. Squires and Ridenour vs. Sanders case
   b. investment portfolio
   c. railroad

5. The last time I went to a halloween party I went _____
   a. as Donald Trump
   b. as Donald Duck
   c. just to please my wife

6. The last time I flew it was _____
   a. on the Concorde to Paris
   b. on a free, frequent-flier ticket to St. Croix
   c. a kite with the kids in the park

7. When relatives come for the weekend, we ask
   a. the cleaning lady to come a day early
   b. for a luxury suite at the Hyatt
   c. the kids to sleep on the familyroom floor

8. The last time I was served dessert at a restaurant
   a. it was on fire
   b. it was made with a yogurt-raspberry whip
   c. it weighed three pounds and was good

9. The last time I talked to my neighbor was
   a. when I circulated a zoning petition to ban basketball poles in neighborhood driveways
   b. when we ran out of Grey Poupon mustard
   c. yesterday, when I helped him install a garage door opener

10. I think that I shall never see
    a. a modern dance recital more exquisite than this
    b. a credit card statement with zero balance due
    c. a foreign movie

11. The last guy out should
    a. turn off the lights in the sauna
    b. tip the limo driver
    c. have waited for a better pitch

12. The last virus that went around at work
    a. destroyed half the files in the computer
    b. hit half the staff the day the boss left town
    c. caused me to stop the truck every 20 minutes

13. "There's something about an __________"
    a. ocean cruise
    b. espresso machine
    c. Aqua Velva man

14. My credit cards ________
    a. outnumber my relatives
    b. have created a debt equal to that of a third-world country
    c. haven't been out of my wallet in over a year

Answers

If you answered anything but "c" to any of the above questions, you're still not very regular. If you didn't figure out that consistent pattern before you were halfway through, you're also not very bright.

Scoring

Give yourself whatever points you want. You deserve them for staying with the book this long. Besides, you don't get a diploma if you pass. You don't even get a free hamburger at the Wendy's restaurant in your area, unless you happen to know Dave Thomas.

Some Clues That You May Not Be Regular

- The only time you were out in the woods, you were with a bunch of guys who paid $300 to chant, beat drums, and listen to poetry.
- You see your kids so seldom that they call you "Uncle Dad."
- Your wife gets ready for work in less time than you.
- You don't know how to start a lawn mower.
- You have his and her closets, each with an individually designed organizer system.
- They're both filled to capacity with clothes.
- You don't carry anything smaller than a $50 bill and you often pay with plastic.
- The only time you were truly relaxed was when they gave you Sodium Pentothal for a face lift.
- At the last party you went to, you stood around drinking sherry and talking about the artistic decadence of 18th century composers.
- You are regularly billed by an art broker, a stock broker, a tailor of custom shirts, a caterer, or a masseur.
- Your dog has a standing appointment with a dog walker.
- Your car license plate number is MBA.
- Your wife's license plate number is MRS MBA.
- You drive from your attached garage at home to the underground parking garage at work and haven't been outdoors in three years.

If you did poorly on the quizzes and figured out that some – or worse, all – of the final clues apply to you, here's what you need to do:

Go out and get yourself some plain, comfortable jeans and a plaid shirt. Take some of your fancy duds down to the Salvation Army for some guys who could really use them. You'll be surprised by the good feeling you get.

From there, go to the store and pick up a six-pack (beer, not mineral water) and a bag of corn chips, pork rinds and/or potato chips. Now, go home and watch a game on television. After that, if you have kids, reintroduce yourself and play a game with them. Better yet, go out in the yard, dig some worms, and take the kids fishing.

Slow down. Relax. Take a snooze.

It's going to take some time, but you can get regular.

There's one more thing you should know about being a regular guy. People are going to be talking about you. They are going to be saying things – things like, "He's a decent sort of guy. Always willing to help out. And friendly, easy to get along with."

"He's down to earth, too. A hard worker. You can count on him."

"He's a real likeable fellow. Easy going. A good Joe."

"Yes, Sir. He's a regular guy."

The Lee Stratton Bio Fact Sheet (or "Why My Wife Swears Her Next Husband Is Going to be Normal...and Rich")

I was born September 3, 1945, in Columbus, Ohio.

I grew up in West Jefferson, Ohio, a small farming community about 10 miles west of the state capital of Columbus—population was about 5,000 at the time. It was a one-cop town with a Dairy Queen restaurant, a movie house, and a drug store with a real soda fountain. My parents still live there. My dad had a sand and gravel and ready-mix concrete company there. He still goes to all the high school football games. Football is a big thing in West Jefferson. My mom still buys me underwear and socks for Christmas.

I graduated from Jefferson Memorial High School in 1963. There were 48 members in the graduating class. Nearly half started the first grade together. The West Jefferson football team was rated first in the state my senior year, but I played in the marching band. I was in the band more than 7 years. We started marching young so they would have enough band members on the football field to form a "J." I played trombone because the trombone players got to march in the front row behind the majorettes.

I didn't go to college. I went to the University of Toledo. I studied to be a music teacher, but my draft board didn't think I was studying hard enough. So I began a three-year enlistment in the Army in 1967, which is how I became a Vietnam vet.

I enrolled at Ohio State University and eventually received my degree in Journalism. My first job was with the Chillicothe *Gazette* in Chillicothe, Ohio.

In 1976 I became a general assignment reporter for the Columbus *Dispatch*. I have covered a number of beats including police, city hall, state government, and public utilities. I am now a feature writer and write a weekly column called "Parenthood." It's been a good job. I've met a lot of interesting and regular people.

Adele and I have been married 19 years. When we go out together, I introduce her as "my first wife."

We have two sons, Brad, 14, and Michael, 8. Brad likes basketball, pizza, peanut butter, and the new *Star Trek* show. Michael likes Cub Scouts, pizza, peanut butter and baseball, and Looney Tunes cartoons. We're raising them regular.

We root for the Ohio State Buckeyes, the Cincinnati Reds, the Columbus Chill hockey team, the Columbus Clippers (AAA farm team of the Yankees), and whatever team Nolan Ryan happens to be playing on since he once had dinner at my house when I was a kid in West Jefferson. Clippers fans are regular folks. They take cow bells to ring during the game. I don't know why, except for it seems like the natural thing to do in Columbus.

We have two cars: a 1979 Plymouth Horizon and a 1985 Plymouth Voyager that I bought used several years ago. We used to have a dog. But he died. I've still got my trombone.